PEOPLE OVER PROPERTY

PEOPLE OVER PROPERTY

HOW TO BUY INVESTMENT PROPERTIES WITHOUT SELLING YOUR SOUL

IAN LEMKE

MANUSCRIPTS
PRESS

PEOPLE OVER PROPERTY

How to Buy Investment Properties without Selling Your Soul

ISBN   979-8-88926-865-9 *Paperback*

979-8-88926-866-6 *Hardcover*

979-8-88926-864-2 *Ebook*

Dedication

Contents

Great returns come because of biblical values—not at the expense of them.

Introduction

Does your faith affect the way you invest? The trickier question is this: How does your faith affect the way you invest?[1]

—HENRY KAESTNER

I began purchasing rental properties for passive income. Period! A few years into my real estate investing career, my wife made it very clear:

"This family needs God!"

She was going to church without me because she was tired of me mocking the music and the message. I eventually began attending out of guilt. In my mind, there was still a clear distinction: church on Sunday, business as usual on Monday.

I ran my business as an all-landlord, no-Christian. I was the typical slumlord and hellbent on generating enough passive income from my rental portfolio to quit my nine-to-five job by any means necessary. *Pay me the rent! That repair is not my responsibility! You're late! If you're not out by Friday, I'm filing an eviction.*

As my property portfolio exploded, people became mere shrapnel!

It didn't take me long to realize not only did my family need God, *my business needed God!*

I began countering this greed by prioritizing people. In every transaction, every investment, and every business decision, how can I prioritize people over money?[2] Real estate became my ministry to honor God and His people.

WHY PEOPLE OVER PROPERTY?

Everyone believes real estate is an asset. In fact, the majority of all millionaires own real estate. Based on my own experience and firsthand interviews, I believe the *real* "asset" in real estate is not the property—it's the people! People are the most valuable asset on your balance sheet. Real estate actually becomes a liability if you fail to see the value of people.

I saw this in my own life when I began renting out my properties and having to evict just a few months later. I was buying investment properties but selling my soul for money. I invested in real estate before I invested in people. Oops!

If people live on the liability ledger of your balance sheet, then your success as an investor will not be fruitful. After all, what good is property without people? Property doesn't pay you; people do.

It wasn't until I began partnering *with* God to purchase properties that I started to see how much impact we have on people as real estate investors. Within one year of establishing this people over property mindset, I doubled my portfolio's size, decreased the number of evictions, and increased the cash flow from each property. Within two years, I quit corporate America and now perform my God-given calling by shepherding people through property.

I began asking God how He wanted me to invest. *Should I invest in this property or that one?* He is now my number one financial consultant. When we allow God to be our financial adviser, everything changes.[3] After all, it's all God's money anyway. I am just the bookkeeper. He provides me with my monthly allowance in the form of rental income.

WHO SHOULD READ THIS

You're likely reading this book because you've always wanted to invest in real estate. Or, you may be investing already and desire to scale your current portfolio. Either way, you're a proven action taker, and it's time to apply that drive and dream bigger.

People over Property is for you if:

- You're ready to invest in real estate but don't know where to start.
- You're already investing in real estate and want to scale your portfolio.
- You are tired of working for someone else and desire to live on your terms.

- You are disciplined: you set goals, develop a plan of action, and make steady progress.
- You are creative, flexible, and willing to adjust your strategy according to the circumstances.
- You have a servant's heart and understand that we prosper through relationships.

People around you may not understand why you're so persistent in your path of progress. They don't realize you're not just working hard for today; your hard work today ensures you don't have to work as hard in five or ten years. You're working on your war chest while your friends are working for the weekend. They're okay with trading hours for dollars in hopes of the big payoff we know as retirement. But you know retirement isn't an age. It's a monthly income.

You also understand that real estate is risky, and some strategies are riskier than others. For me, working for someone else for thirty to forty years—not being able to express my own creativity and earn a living that was both stimulating and fulfilling—was even riskier! I didn't like the idea of saving my way to retirement. I wanted to experience life now while I'm in my prime—not when I'm too old to enjoy it! The riskiest thing we can do is to play it safe. When we avoid risks, we often end up avoiding what God is doing in the world.[4] We're never going to eliminate sin from our portfolios. We just can't. As long as we are investing in people on this side of heaven, we are investing in sinners,[5] myself included!

But getting started in real estate is easier than you think. There is a specific method for you based on the amount of money you have, your tolerance to risk, and the time you want to commit. You really just have to select one strategy and stick with it.

As the ideal reader, you see that ultimate freedom is not just financial freedom. It's time freedom. You honor your time, and you deserve to get it back! The book you're about to read was made possible by the time freedom that real estate investing created for me. And it can do the exact same for you!

People over Property is not for you if:

- You enjoy your current job and are okay with saving your way to retirement.
- You're risk-averse and cannot fathom the thought of losing money.
- You believe reading one book without subsequent action will bring you financial freedom.
- You believe your work and faith are separate and can be turned on and off like a light switch as you leave one room and enter another.
- You are easily offended by any reference to God or Christianity.

The principles in each chapter are taken from the parables of Jesus; however, you do not need to be a Christian to appreciate the message. The principles laid out in each chapter are broad enough that anyone in any walk of faith can understand and implement them. For example…

In Matthew 13: 31–32, Jesus described the Kingdom of Heaven as a tiny mustard seed planted in the field. It is the smallest of all seeds but becomes the largest of plants and grows into a tree where birds can come and find shelter.[6] Our investment portfolio starts the same way: with one property.

Yet even before we acquire our first property, we have to start with the person: you. You desire to build a life on your terms by helping people who need to sell or desire to buy. That tiny little desire can grow into an enormous tree, yielding the sweetest fruit you'll ever taste—freedom!

Naturally, before it can produce any fruit, the desire must be planted in the right soil (principles), watered with the Word (prayer), fertilized with learning (education), warmed with wisdom (action), and trimmed by the blade of discernment (reflection). With enough time and attention, the people in your community find shelter in the branches of your rental homes.

MY PROMISE TO YOU

I promise if you leverage the tools provided in this book, by this time next year, you will be on your way to building a new career, a new lifestyle, a new portfolio of property, and an eternity filled with prosperity. With this book, you can build a legitimate business, a lifestyle, a legacy, and a lifetime stream of income, all while simultaneously serving the Lord.

The biggest takeaway you'll gain is how to invest (with God) by helping both sellers and buyers in your own backyard or thousands of miles away and repeat it over and over until your monthly passive income exceeds your active income from your current job.

Sure, you can passively read this. I'll do my best to entertain and engage you. But I don't believe you picked up this book to be entertained. You could've easily turned on your television, but you didn't. You've selected this book because you want to learn how to invest in real estate. Yet, if all you gained were a few hours of entertainment after reading this book, and your only action was, "Hmph… that's interesting," then I've failed you, my friend. Conversely, if your reading leads to massive action, then mission accomplished.

Most people want to earn their four-year degree in real estate in the first year. That makes no sense. You would never go into college and say, "If I can't make this degree in one year, this doesn't work. I want my money back." Yet, so many people I know who began investing gave up too soon before their mustard seed had time to sprout.

So, I must ask: What if, in six months, you have your first investment property? What if it takes nine months? Twelve? Would it be worth it? What if, over the next five years, you've built a portfolio of property that gave all your time back? Would it be worth it? I don't know. Only you can answer that: *What is the next twenty to thirty years of your life worth?*

PEOPLE OVER PROPERTY BLUEPRINT

Each chapter contains a parable of Jesus and how I see it relates to my walk as a faith-driven investor. You'll see how these parables relate to how we can honor people and build a profitable portfolio. I recommend you read in sequential order to not miss the point made in each chapter. You may be tempted to skip straight to the property section to learn the how-to. However, fair warning, I did this in my career and suffered the consequences by valuing property more than people—an expensive price to pay!

I laid out this book in four sections: prayer, people, property, and prosperity.

SECTION ONE: PRAYER

Chapters one and two are the first phase in which we lay the *foundation*. You'll learn my path away from God and what brought me back to Him. You'll learn how I failed my way through my first property and how I've learned to include God in my business.

SECTION TWO: PEOPLE

Chapters three through seven are the second phase, where we begin to *rough-in* the premise of valuing people more than property. These chapters describe the key players in your portfolio: sellers, tenants, and tenant-buyers.

SECTION THREE: PROPERTY

Chapters eight through ten are the third phase, where we'll frame the *structural* components of each investment strategy. There is more than one way to skin a cat and even more ways to serve people through property. These chapters have heavily weighted how-tos. Pay special attention and take good notes.

Chapters eleven and twelve are the final *top-out* phase. You'll learn the six ways an investment portfolio pays you. You'll also learn how to carry forward this new people over property mindset as you create financial freedom, time freedom, and peace of mind freedom.

Real estate investing will provide passive profits that can fertilize your future fields of freedom. I wanted this for myself when I first began. And I want this even more for you. More importantly, I want you to learn how to buy investment properties without *selling your soul*!

Let's begin.

SECTION ONE:

PRAYER

CHAPTER 1:

The Power of Prayer

—

Prayer is the most wonderful experience man can have.[1]

—NEVILLE GODDARD

THE DAY I QUIT CHRIST

I was thirteen years old when I gave up on Christianity.

My parents tried to instill Christian values in my life. However, with enough rebellion, I was given a get-out-of-church-free card in my adolescent years. I didn't really understand prayer. I certainly didn't respect it. At age thirteen, I didn't know prayer's power and importance.

I was raised as a Christian but never really understood the Bible or prayer. My sisters and I attended church but did not connect with the teachings. My father was raised Lutheran and my mother Baptist. They were classic flower child hippies who grew up in the 1960s. They *believed,* but they gravitated more toward the *spiritual* teachings of the world. My mother despised the church, but she placated my father because he knew my sisters and I needed it.

I certainly didn't want church. I made sure to express my disinterest every Sunday. I envied my neighborhood friends who didn't have to go. Man, how lucky they were! Finally, after several years of complaining, my parents gave me a hall pass and said I no longer had to attend church. *Praise the Lord. I'm finally free!*

While visiting my grandparents that summer, we sat down for lunch on their back porch one afternoon. The townhome in which they lived overlooked a luscious green golf course. Grandpa began to mumble under his breath, though I couldn't make out the words. My sister and I looked at each other in confusion. I started mumbling gibberish just like Grandpa—hoping to get a laugh out of my sister. What I experienced instead was the cold sting of my grandpa's wedding ring as he backhanding me across the face. *Whack!*

"You think it's funny to make fun of prayer, huh? Yeah... real funny to make fun of prayer!" he exclaimed.

Just a few seconds of blasphemy was all Grandpa would allow. He hit me so hard that his wedding ring gave me a fat lip! I was shocked. I'd never been hit with such force. I felt the physical pain, but the emotional pain is what penetrated me the most.

My grandpa hit me. Is he allowed to do that? He isn't my father. Who is he to discipline me? And what did I do wrong anyway? I pondered.

In an instant, all my fondest memories of playing with Grandpa in my youth vanished and were replaced with feelings of anger and resentment. Even up to his passing when I was twenty-eight years old, I truly hadn't forgiven him. However, holding that anger and frustration inside was not serving me. It's not like my grandpa knew he'd scarred me emotionally. He probably never gave it a second thought. Yet, I was allowing this scene, which lasted no longer than a split second, to impact me well into my adult life! Why?

My grandpa was living rent-free in my mind, more commonly referred to as *squatting*!

My mortgage company doesn't let me live in my house for free, nor do my tenants stay in my properties rent-free. So, why was I allowing this one small moment in my adolescent years to prevent me from tapping into the power of prayer?

I was at that pivotal age of thirteen when puberty set in, moral values strengthened, and the need for independence rose. From that point on, I made up my own version of what God is and gravitated to more worldly viewpoints and spiritual beliefs.

SAND SCRIPT

Wayne Dyer was my very first introduction to personal development. Growing up, my father would listen to cassette tapes on our long road trips in our 1970s brown station wagon. Fast forward to the age of twenty-four, when I was offered a job in the sales department: I had no sales experience, so I bought as many books as possible.

Remembering my father's old tape sets, I rushed to find them in storage, dusted them off, and quickly began listening. Here's the irony: at age ten, riding in the back seat of the station wagon, I was pleading *no more*; at age twenty-four, I was begging *more, more!* In one of his stories, Wayne gave his patient a simple homework assignment:

> Go to the beach, close your eyes, and just listen. Listen to the ocean; listen to the seagulls; listen to the sounds of children playing; just listen. Then, go to the water's edge. Write your worries in the sand and watch how quickly they disappear.[2]

That idea intrigued me. However, I was living in Albuquerque, New Mexico— hundreds of miles from any ocean. Nevertheless, the story stuck. Years later, I had the opportunity to travel to Mexico for a four-day beach getaway. While walking along the beach with my wife, Lynn, Wayne Dyer's story came back to me. With the energy of a small child, I rushed to find the nearest piece of beach wood as a writing tool. Instead of writing my *worries*, I began writing what I desired. Lynn, puzzled by my excitement, asked what in the world I was doing. She reluctantly chose to play along.

At the time, we were both frustrated and unfulfilled in our work. She was a teacher; I was an insurance claims adjuster. We had been applying to multiple jobs in multiple fields but were declined at every turn. So, we both decided to write "new job" in the sand and took a picture of it. We sat on the beach and watched as the rising tide slowly carried away our desire—letter by letter.

"It's now in the hands of the abundant ocean," I explained.

It was hard to tell if Lynn was buying it or if she believed in the process at all was hard to tell. I can't blame her for having doubts. After all, I didn't even know if it'd work! Three weeks after returning home, I landed an interview, which led to an offer as a stockbroker *plus* a 15 percent pay raise! Two weeks after my interview, Lynn received an offer outside of her teaching field that included a 20 percent increase in pay!

Maybe there was something to this intention-setting business. Was all this predetermined to unfold regardless of Wayne Dyer's simple sand script simulation? Were our new jobs always available to us, and we just had to focus our attention in the right direction? Was this sand script a prayer to the universe, to the ocean, or to God? Was it fate? Destiny? We didn't know at the time. Either way, we were elated!

Now, every time we go to the beach, I write dozens of requests, desires, and outcomes. And yes, *author* was one of those requests; *retiring Lynn* was another; *full-time entrepreneur* yet another; as well as *coach*, *mentor*, and *trainer*. All these requests became my reality with the power of intention-setting and leveraging the ocean of abundance. I now see these were all prayer requests to God. I asked, and He answered.

As my walk in faith has strengthened, my sand script is now tailored more toward character traits I seek to embody and less about material possessions. My favorite sand script phrases are, "God will provide," and "Ask, and it is given." These remind me to ask for what I want versus complaining about what is. I am grateful God reintroduced me to Wayne Dyer and that his legendary words are still impacting people years after his passing.

SOWING TOGETHER SELF-HELP AND SPIRITUALITY

In Matthew 13:1–23, Jesus shares a parable about a farmer who was planting seeds in his field to illustrate how God's Word impacts different people. Some seeds were eaten up by birds, while other seeds fell on rocky soil, so they didn't get a chance to sprout. Other seeds fell on shallow soil and shot up quickly. The hot sun scorched them; they withered and died, for they had so little root. Still, other seeds fell among thorns and were choked out. But some fell on good soil and produced a crop that was thirty, sixty, and even one hundred times as much as the farmer planted.[3]

The sequential order of these seeds is intentional: It represents the path of embracing Him. I have embodied each type of seed in my adult life.

- Before Christ, I would brush off anything religious. Birds of essentialism or spirituality would eat me up.
- As I began attending church with my wife, my arms were crossed. So, the rocky soil wasn't fertile enough to penetrate.
- As my faith matured, a message would begin to sink in, but the hot sun of my own ego would scorch the Word.
- Business began to grow, and the thorns of selfish financial gain choked out any possible persuasion.

- Only after embracing God with full faith and trust could the seeds of His Word fall deep into fertile soil to yield one hundred times more than what was planted.

A PRAYER FOR FORGIVENESS

Now, in my forties, as I reflect on the incident with my grandpa, I know this resentment was not isolated only to my grandfather but to the *entire* institution of faith! I avoided anything that had the fragrance of faith. I vowed never to be one of *those* people. And in that process, I shut myself out from allowing the Holy Spirit to flow through me. I built a barricade that insulated myself from God.

The experience drew up a boundary line not only between me and my grandfather but also between me and Jesus. This boundary was causing me bondage in the form of self-pity, anger, and remorse. I had to reconcile with my grandpa. But how could I? He'd passed away years ago. I had to forgive… not only my grandpa but also myself.

Reconciliation requires two people. Luckily, forgiveness only requires one.[4] If we don't forgive someone, we choose to stay in a relationship with them. They're still playing a toxic role in our lives. Forgiveness is freedom.[5] If I forgave him, I would be set free. I prayed that God would release this anger I held toward my grandpa.

I prayed I might remember the fun of roughhousing with Grandpa instead of that moment when I gave up on him and lost confidence in the *faith*. I prayed my heart would open and allow love to flow in. Slowly, over time, God has answered my prayers. I can now reflect on my memories of Grandpa with love and joy.

PRAY PERSISTENTLY

In Luke 11:5–13, Jesus explains if you go to a friend's house at midnight asking for food, your friend would likely inform you it's late and he can't help you right now. If you are persistent in your request, "He will give you everything you want—just because of your persistence."[6] Jesus instructed His disciples to continually ask for daily bread and to be confident in seeking God to meet their daily needs. The same applies for us.

Jesus also teaches us boundaries. One of the boundaries He communicated indirectly was making time for personal prayer. On several occasions, Jesus would go into the wilderness to be with His Father—even in times when His disciples needed Him the most. Very early in the morning, while it was still dark, Jesus got up, left the house, and went off to a solitary place, where He prayed. When you pray, go away by yourself, all alone, and shut the door behind you and pray to your Father secretly, and your Father, who knows your secrets, will reward you.[7]

Pray for anything. And if you believe, you have it; it's yours.[8] The seemingly harmless habit of "talking to yourself" is the most fruitful form of prayer.[9] Prayer is the art of believing what is denied by the senses.[10] Prayer occurs when we depend on God. Prayerlessness occurs when we depend on ourselves.[11]

So, even when we're on the mountaintop, and things are going well, we must keep our focus on Him by continuing to look up for guidance. Otherwise, we may begin to think we can do it ourselves and neglect our Father who art in heaven. "This keeps our egos from inflating too much during seasons of prosperity, and it prevents bitterness and despondency in times of adversity."[12]

By this point, you might be asking: *What does any of this have to do with investing in real estate, people, or properties?* You want to invest in real estate? Create cash flow? Provide for your family? Impact the lives of others? You want to buy investment properties without selling your soul?

It all starts with a prayer.

CHAPTER 2

The Property without a Prayer

———

Most people think buying is investing, but they're wrong [it] doesn't make you an investor any more than buying groceries makes you a chef.[1]

—GARY KELLER

I began investing in real estate before investing in Christ.

I didn't have a people over property mindset when I invested in my first rental. People were like pawns to be played in the game of property chess. My principle was property over people. *People stay in my property and serve me,* I rationalized. I was quick to judge. I was over critical and insincere. I wasn't even a practicing Christian, yet I exuded a holier-than-thou demeanor to my tenants.

THE PROPERTY WITHOUT A PRAYER

I purchased my first rental property on October 31, 2017, using traditional financing. I was anxious to get a tenant in and was freaking out about having to pay the first month's mortgage. After plenty of showings, no one was biting. Month two came, and I had to pay another month's mortgage payment! *When am I going to start cash-flowing?*

After screening several dozen renter prospects, I noticed a pattern among these prospects and began categorizing them into three buckets:

- Qualified
- Quirky
- Quack

Qualified tenants pay their bills on time. They have great jobs and good credit. They could probably buy their own house, yet they simply choose to rent. Quirky tenants are also good people. But they may have a small blemish on their record—enough to scare off other landlords (i.e., high student loan balances or medical bills, vicious dog breed owner, experienced a divorce which led to a repossession of a vehicle or an eviction). Finally, quacks are the people who cannot verify any income, have no steady job, or have a colorful criminal history. Quacks have cash and need to move in fast!

Obviously, you always look for the qualified tenants:

- Credit score of 620-plus
- Twelve months of steady, verifiable income that exceeds three times the monthly rent payment

- No felonies, evictions, bankruptcies, or repossessions on their record

Most people have something in their past they're not proud of. Lord knows I do. I led a life of sin before coming to Christ—and even after. It'd be foolish to think we can hedge against all sin in our investing portfolio. Author Luke Roush says, "As long as we were investing on this side of heaven, we are investing in sinners."[2]

It's not that you can't rent to the quirkies or the quacks. It's a matter of how much security deposit they pay to compensate for the risk they bear. Quirkies and quacks will pay a premium because they have no other choice: no other landlord will rent to them. As sinister as this sounds, I'd like to share just a small sample of what I experienced in my first rental property so you can get a taste of the three tenant flavors.

THE QUACK

Desperate and anxious to not have to pay a third month's mortgage, the first tenants I selected were quacks! Their background check showed several missed credit card payments and an eviction. But people can change, right? The husband now had a job in the oil fields, making good money. Surely it wouldn't be a problem.

Well, every month, it became a struggle to collect rent. They hadn't paid on time nor in full even once. I rationalized their behavior as, *They're paying all the late fees each time—no big deal.* Each month their excuses became more creative and harder to challenge, at least, not without me sounding like a heartless slumlord.

"I was sick and didn't get enough hours at work."
"Our kid's doctor bills…"
"I had to pay my attorney, or else I'd lose my visitation rights with my daughter."

One afternoon, I visited the property to do a minor repair and found the tenant intoxicated from what appeared to be alcohol—but was later revealed to be heroin. Puddles of puppy urine were throughout our brand-new vinyl plank flooring. The house reeked of puppy pee! I didn't know what to say, so I said nothing. I finished the repair and left in shock.

How could people live like that? I thought.

As the months went on, the payments seemed to come later and later. I was not abiding by the *no pay, no stay* policy. I found myself sticking up for the tenants and having empathy for them. One month, I even told my wife, "Hey, honey, I'm sorry. We can't go out to eat this week. But I'm letting my tenants stay in the house for free."

My wife had finally had enough. We needed to get them out! I placed a seventy-two-hour notice to vacate on the inside of the front door.

The tenant called me, screaming, "You can't do this! I'm not leaving. You'll have to evict me!" Thankfully, I kept my composure.

"You're right. I will evict. This is your three-day courtesy notice to leave to avoid an eviction filing on your record," I said.

"That's bull! I know the law. I'm not leaving!" he said as he hung up.

After three days, he didn't leave—shocker! I filed for eviction that Monday and had a court date scheduled two weeks later. At court, I approached the judge to explain, "My tenant owes $1,400 plus $200 in late fees. We request possession of the property."

"Do you agree that you owe this amount?" the judge asked the wife.

"Yes, but…"

"… and can you pay this amount?" The judge jumped in before she had a chance to explain.

"No."

"Then, you have five days to vacate the property. If you aren't out in five days, we will have a sheriff come to the property and move your belongings to the curb. The landlord will have the locks changed," the judge explained.

This was music to my ears!

On the sixth day, my wife and I returned to the property. There were no cars out front. As we entered the property, the only thing the tenants left was the rank smell of dog urine on our new floors.

As we assessed the minor damage on the first floor, I heard sounds coming from upstairs. Halfway up the stairwell, I encountered a heroin junkie and his girlfriend squatting in the house! *What?*

As shaken up as I was, I kept my cool. The intruder was a pail, frail man blasted out of his mind on heroin, so there was no confrontation. I gently explained we were the owners and that we'd come to take possession of the property. He sheepishly gathered his items and handed me the keys along with the remote to the garage door opener where he was hiding his car.

Now, all that was left in the house was a putrid smell of dog urine. I ended up replacing the carpet upstairs but managed to salvage the plank flooring downstairs. I scrubbed and scrubbed—but still never managed to remove the odor completely. My lease now states that all dogs must be twelve months or older and be house-trained. It was a costly lesson to learn.

THE QUIRKY

With my bank account even more in the red, I quickly backfilled the property with a quirky tenant. She was self-employed with no verifiable income other than several months of bank statements showing large cash deposits. We hedged our risk by collecting twice the standard deposit amount.

She loved the house and stayed there for three years with only one late payment. She asked if she could make her own improvements to the storage shed in the backyard. About halfway through the second year, she asked if we'd sell her the house using owner financing.

At this point, I had owned the property for four years and paid down a sizable portion of the mortgage balance. Also, the market price for the property increased substantially within that time. So, before selling the tenant the property, I refinanced the current loan to capture the equity that had built up.

"We'll send an appraiser next week to obtain the current value of the property," I advised.

"I probably should have told you earlier. But I've remodeled the property substantially over the past year when you said you'd sell it to me. I don't want to be charged an even higher purchase price for the work I've done," she pleaded.

My wife almost lost it. *She did what? We don't even have a signed contract. We never even gave her a contract. Now, she thinks she can remodel our house without asking us?*

You can learn a lot about your tenants by simply following them on social media. I learned she had given birth to two children naturally *in my bathtub*! She also posted that she had two parakeets, four cats, three dogs, and a hedgehog. I was only aware of (and only charging pet rent for) two dogs and one cat.

The final straw was when the appraiser arrived, and the tenant refused to let him in!

I rescheduled the appraisal appointment for a week later when the tenant wasn't there, and she changed the locks! It was obvious she had to go. A few days later, I confronted her in person to advise her that not only would we *not* be selling her the property, but we would also *not* renew her lease. She must use these next four months to find a new place to live.

"You can't do this! I'm not leaving. You'll have to evict me!"

Oh, boy. This again?

On the last day of her lease, I got a call from a neighbor indicating that water from my property was flooding into her yard. The tenant intentionally sabotaged my property! I dropped what I was doing and raced to assess the damage. I pictured the worst: all sinks and tubs stopped up with water flooding the entire place, and I had no key to get in!

Thankfully, it was only an exterior hose spigot just outside of the garage. I turned off the water and called the plumber. Since I was already at the property, I might as well begin changing the locks. But, with no key, what do I do—break a window? Thankfully, but also peculiar, the back door was unlocked. She already removed most of her property. The only things remaining were old sheets, pillows, and some other junk.

While changing the locks, random people were driving by, giving me awkward stares. One person even approached me, stating she was there to pick up some sheets. She showed me my tenant's social media post claiming a free-for-all. After another half dozen awkward stares from others, the tenant called me.

"Are you at the house?" she asked.

"Yes. I'm changing the locks because your lease is up," I replied.

"You have no right to be there. I'm calling the police!" she said.

Within fifteen minutes, the police arrived. "Why are you changing the locks today if her lease isn't up until tomorrow?" the policeman asked.

"Is it a coincidence that on the final day of the lease, the hose spigot breaks in half, and the neighbor calls me in frantic?" I questioned.

"No. Probably not a coincidence," he confessed.

The policeman was now beginning to see the tenant's quirkiness.

But, to keep the peace, the policeman informed me, "You must give her until 11:59 p.m. tonight. If she is not out by tomorrow, call me back, reference this case number, and I will help remove her."

The next day, I was relieved to find that everything the tenant had affixed to the property was still in place. She had also swept and mopped the entire house. She was out! I was incredibly grateful this rollercoaster ride was over. The whole experience left me drained—hoping I'd never have to go through something like this again.

At this point, I was zero to two and not sure how I could make a comeback.

THE CHARACTER CHANGE

"What's wrong with this house?" I asked my wife.

It's in a good area and a good school district with good neighbors. Plus, it's in good condition and had good bones.

Maybe this house was a lame duck instead of a golden goose. *Should I just sell it? Cash in my chips? Cut my losses? No. I couldn't sell now. I had just refinanced and spent $14,000 in closing costs!*

That night, as I lay in bed, I asked myself a different question. *What's wrong with me?*

Up to this point, I'd been trying to find a solution on my own. I wasn't leveraging my mentors, nor was I leaning into the power of prayer. It took four years of investing in real estate and going through these two terrible experiences to realize I must also invest in God. One of my consistent failures in the face of ethical tensions is to assume that somehow determining the correct resolution is up to me. I reminisced on how terrible these past two experiences went.

"What are we going to do?" I asked my wife.

Lynn's response was brilliant: "This house needs prayer!"

"That's it!" I exclaimed.

That's what had been missing. I purchased this property in 2017. But it wasn't until 2021 I began following Christ. I never asked God to bless this house. After all, God has the ability to grant miracles! Why not tap into some of His power? We can approach His throne knowing that if we ask, He will answer. So, why not ask? He answers those who ask.[3] John 16:24 says, "You have not done this before. Ask, using my name, and you will receive, and you will have abundant joy."[4]

I prayed God would send the right prospect at the right time, with the right qualifications and the right circumstances. I prayed diligently over the next two weeks.

THE QUALIFIED

During those next two weeks of praying, the only prospects expressing interest were more quacks! Still, my prayers continued. I prayed in the morning in bed. I prayed on my morning walk. I prayed at lunch. I prayed at dinner and before bed. I asked everyone I knew to pray. There's power in prayer. If we want to see power, we must see prayer.[5]

Yet, I got it wrong. I was making prayer about me instead of about God. I looked to prayer to get what I wanted. Prayer occurs when you depend on God. Praylessness occurs when you depend on yourself.[6] If I prayed long enough, believed enough, and gathered enough others to join, just maybe I'd get what I wanted. I turned prayer on its head and wondered why it didn't work very well. Prayer from the beginning is about God. It is recognizing yourself to be that which you desire to be rather than begging God for that which you desire.[7]

Now, I don't think He minds our praying about things if we leave it at that. What He minds, and opposes steadily, is the prayer that prays on until it is prayed through, assured of the answer.[8] I was looking to God to do all the work while I remained passive. But passivity never pays off. Prayer is powerful. Yet, it's what we do after we pray that determines whether we believe the prayer. God works best when we're in motion. It's easier for Him to steer a moving ship.

In that moment, I prayed for a new beginning—a fresh start as well as a change of heart. Yes, I prayed for a qualified tenant. But more importantly, I prayed God would help shift my perception. I wanted to view people as He sees them: as His own assets that produce fruit.

God wants us to succeed, but on His time, not ours; in His will, not ours. It'd be easier if we could just calibrate our clocks with God's time zone, but that's not the way God intends it for us. All this time, I was praying for outcomes; for results. But that's not really the purpose of prayer. God was showing me He wanted more of His presence within *me*. My prayers began to shift. I prayed for God to grant me the ability to seek Him first; to do what pleases Him. I let go of the outcome and instead asked for God's love to come out of me. What that meant was to serve others around me. So, that is what I did. I carved out time to be with my wife. I spent time helping my children. I prayed for friends who were struggling. I did things I'd been "too busy" for.

Four days later, a large family inquired about the property. They'd just moved back to Texas from Arizona. The husband had a steady, well-paying job, and they absolutely loved the place! Their credit and background check came back flawless. At last, I'd found my *qualified* family!

PERSISTENT IN PRAYER

In Luke 18:1–8, Jesus illustrates a story of the need for constant prayer and to keep praying until the answer comes.[9] A widow was seeking justice against a man who had harmed her,[10] and she repeatedly appealed her case in front of a city judge. The judge ignored her request until, one day, he finally caved. "I'm going to see that she gets justice, for she is wearing me out with her constant coming."[11] The parable teaches us to pray continuously and never give up, even when we face obstacles. "Don't you think God will surely give justice to His people who plead with Him day and night?"[12]

I've now learned to consult with God each morning through prayer before my feet ever hit the ground. It's become more like a conversation with a partner. I ask what He wants of me on this day. Whom must I serve well? Who needs grace? Who needs truth? What action do I need to take? What is the next right move? If I'm wise, I listen.

I believe God really enjoys making marvelous things happen, using the humble… Then it's obvious who, exactly, made that marvelous thing happen. It happened because God will use anybody with a willing heart.[13] And the humble open their heart through prayer.

SECTION TWO:

PEOPLE

CHAPTER 3

Leave the 99, Find the 1 Percent

It's never about the house. It's always about the person and their situation.[1]

—PACE MORBY

LOST SHEEP

"If a man has a hundred sheep, and one wanders away and is lost, what will he do? Won't he leave the ninety-nine others and go out into the hills to search for the lost one? And if he finds it, I tell you the truth, he will rejoice over it more than over the ninety-nine others safe at home!"[2] God is seeking out those who are lost, and He rejoices when they are found.

For many years, I was that lost sheep—both in business and in faith. I was raised Christian but fell into more worldly views in my teenage years. I was consumed by greed, money, and ill-gotten gain. My win meant your loss.

I stumbled upon God through my real estate investing business. He talked to me through my transactions. He'd cause me to ask: *Is this deal helping the seller or just helping me?* This was the reality check I needed! As my faith grew, so did my business. Shocking! I know. Although I still fall off track daily, God is able to help guide me back on the right path and rejoices when I return.

I relate this parable of the lost sheep to the sellers we serve. The mission of my investment company is to *help sellers out and help buyers in:* help sellers out of a tight spot and help buyers into a home they never thought possible. This has become a very narrow niche: the 1 percent.

I'm willing to leave the ninety-nine that don't resonate with my offer and rejoice when I find the one. I aim to close 1 percent of the warm leads that raise their hand asking for help. Meaning I'll never do business with 99 percent of the people who respond to my advertising. It's my job (and yours) to find the 1 percent who may have lost their way.

How often have you driven by a billboard for a restaurant you'll never visit? How many times have you seen a commercial of an injury attorney screaming, "Call today!" yet you've never called? How many ads do you scroll past on your phone each day but never click? Have you ever responded to one of those direct mail campaigns? I haven't. Why? You and I are not their 1 percent. Rather, were the other ninety-nine sheep. Those advertisers aren't looking for me.

They're willing to spend 100 percent of their time and money focusing on finding their 1 percent. You and I should be doing the same in our real estate prospecting.

The seller I'm seeking has tried everything to sell their home but with no success. They have given up and need guidance. I talk to one hundred sellers in search of the one who can truly benefit from my creative offer.

Table 3.1 below summarizes the specific set of seller's circumstances you and I should be listening for:

SELLER'S CIRCUMSTANCES		
Very little equity in the house; fair market value = mortgage balance	Not looking to purchase another house right away	Already have a another place to move/live
Realistic about the property value	Tried listing it but no success	Tired of dealing with flakey buyers
Property has deferred maintenance and needs work	Unable to make the repairs	Bought another house and can't afford two mortgages
Prefer a quick, hassle-free sale	Behind on mortgage payments; possibly facing foreclosure	Behind on property taxes
No money to pay an agent or closing costs	Emotionally "done" with the property	Bad blood with their tenant

Does this list seem a bit predatory? Potentially.

This industry is plagued with opportunistic investors who capitalize on others' misfortunes. Many of the sellers I've spoken to have shared how cold other investors are. They tell me how other investors offered them only 50 percent of what their property was worth. Others have said they're being rushed out of their own home!

However, if you show up as someone who can help, and if your approach resonates with them, then it's no longer zero-sum game (i.e., your gain at their loss). It can truly be a win-win arrangement. You help them avoid foreclosure by catching up their payments; they save their credit score. You pay all the closing costs; they get this financial or emotional burden off their back. You give them all the time they need to move out; they don't have to make any repairs. And you offer them full market price using creative financing (discussed in chapter nine).

You win because they win!

CHASING SHEEP

After wasting thousands of hours and marketing dollars chasing down prospective sellers, I've learned it's so much easier to have sellers come to me. In the beginning, I would purchase lists of property owners, send direct mail, and make every effort to contact them by phone or email, only to be told to get lost!

So, where are all these sellers who need our help? Where is anyone nowadays? On the internet. They're scrolling through Facebook or Instagram. They're watching videos on YouTube or TikTok. They're on Google searching for ways to sell their house fast. If you can be the first investor they see on any of these platforms, they'll ask if *you* will buy *their* house. Your answer should always be: "Yes, with the right terms."

In your ad, you state you can pay full market price for their house. They're intrigued. They raise their hand; they complete the property intake form; they schedule a call; they show up for the call; and they're open to hear your unique offer because they've already heard most other lowball offers.

Those who don't? Well, you and I don't buy. They're part of the ninety-nine who are well-fed and have other options to sell their house.

I NEVER SAW A SIGN!

Thousands of properties are sold every day without ever going on the market—no "for sale" sign needed. In this digital age, some sellers are more comfortable selling to iBuyers (or instant buyers) on the internet than through traditional face-to-face methods. It's easier, faster, and, overall, more convenient. Think about it: When you're purchasing a car, do you go straight to the car dealership? Or do you shop online at your convenience, find the exact car you want, then—and only then—reach out to the dealer? Sellers are more honest online than they are in person when it comes to things like the condition of the home, the lowest price they'd accept, and so on.

Instant buyers like OpenDoor, Zillow, Sundae, and OfferPad have invested billions of dollars into making it easier than ever to sell your house online. One of my realtor friends chose to sell her own residence to an iBuyer out of sheer convenience, even though she could have listed her house herself and earned a commission. People are willing to compromise for convenience and speed!

CONNECTING BUYERS AND SELLERS—NO REAL ESTATE LICENSE REQUIRED

People have asked me: "Do you have your real estate license?" No. I don't need one. It's true: You must have a license if you're connecting buyers and sellers for a profit. But you're not the middleman here. You're not making money from connecting buyers and sellers. You *are* the buyer. Real estate agents are great at finding houses. But what if you could find these houses yourself? What if sellers come to you asking if you'll buy their property? Obviously, not many will. But we're looking for the one out of a hundred who happens to be lost. Their circumstances have led them astray, and they've exhausted all their options.

So, how do you know if you're dealing with the 1 percent versus the 99 percent?

THE 99 PERCENT

One hundred percent of the inbound seller leads who respond to my advertisements ask if I will buy their house. And my answer is always: *Yes… with the right terms.* I will give you your asking price but on my terms. Or I'll give you your terms but with my asking price. This doesn't resonate well with 99 percent of these sellers. They want it all. The following are snippets of conversations I've had with the 99 percent of people I'll never do business with:

"Is the option of owner financing on the table," I asked.

"Why would I finance your business?" he replied. Ninety-nine.

"Would you be open to working out a creative purchase arrangement?" I inquired.

"Sure. Give me a 50 percent down payment so I can pay off my mortgage, and we can work out the rest on a monthly payment basis," she answered. Ninety-nine.

"Once you buy my house and catch up on my mortgage payments, I'd like to continue living in it for the next few years." Ninety-nine.

"I'm a real estate broker, and I am trying to sell my primary residence. I need you to pay me 6 percent commissions when you buy my house." Ninety-nine!

"I'm in foreclosure. The auction date is set for next week with the auction price of $100,000. I'll sell it to you for $250,000." Ninety-nine.

"My tenant pays me $1,000, and he wants to stay after I sell. Can you buy it, and he continues to pay *me* the $1,000 a month?" Ninety-nine.

"Can you buy a new house for me, and I'll give you this one?" Ninety-nine!

As humorous as these sound, they are real responses I received from real (unmotivated) sellers. Of course, determining whether you're dealing with the 99 or the 1 percent isn't always as obvious as these extreme examples mentioned above.

However, you can allow automation to help you work through the weeds and whittle down to the 1 percent. That way, the 99 can continue to graze in the grass with the rest of the herd. You allow the 99 percent to screen themselves out through the natural flow of your automated sequence.

Remember, you're only looking for the 1 percent.

THE 1 PERCENT

As of this writing, I'm working with a seller in Pennsylvania who'd checked all the boxes we mentioned previously in table 3.1.

- Not looking to purchase another house or already has another place to live
- Realistic about the property value
- Tried listing it but with no success
- Property has deferred maintenance and is unable to make the repairs
- Has two mortgages and is unable to pay both each month
- Prefers a quick, hassle-free sale
- Behind on mortgage payments and taxes, facing foreclosure
- Emotionally done with the property
- Bad blood with the tenant

She was definitely in a tight spot and needed guidance. Her biggest pain was that she had a squatting rent-to-own tenant who hadn't made a payment in nine months! She was going broke trying to pay her own mortgage along with this rental property's mortgage. She tried to sell it before, but her rent-to-own tenant made it so difficult that the two prior buyers backed out.

I fully understood her position.

Her mortgage balance is $75,000, and the property value is $300,000. She was initially asking $150,000, which I'd be more than willing to pay if the circumstances were different. It wouldn't be an issue if I could get a licensed home inspector in to do a top-to-bottom inspection and get a professional photographer to take pictures. But with her squatting tenant in the mix, neither of these were feasible.

Her tenant will likely cause damage once I evict him, even if it's just to spite the seller. Knowing this, the seller and I approximated what the house could be worth in its current (undamaged) condition. We also approximated the damage her tenant may cause and calculated costs for each of these repairs.

"If I am going to inherit the risk of purchasing a house I've never seen, pay your back taxes, evict your tenant, and make repairs your tenant causes, I'm unable to pay your asking price of $150,000," I explained.

She fully understood my position.

As I lay in bed that night, I asked myself: *Is this the best possible solution for the seller? Is this deal helping the seller or just helping me?* Thankfully, in this case, I truly believe that each of us will walk away feeling like we got what we wanted. It's not a compromised solution, but a true win-win.

I agreed to purchase the property as-is, catch up on her mortgage payments, pay her back taxes, and remove her difficult tenant, even though I've never seen the property. I'm willing to take on this risk because we agreed to a purchase price that equaled her mortgage balance of $75,000, and the property valuation is $300,000.

No arm wrestling. No coercion.

I will purchase this property with less than $2,500 of my own cash out of pocket. No partners. No private lenders. No primary mortgages. In chapter nine, I'll show you how you can do the same. So, stay tuned.

The next chapter will stretch this "us versus them" stigma that currently exists between a buyer and a seller. Rather than treating your sellers as adversaries who must be taken down, you see them as a partner who will bend over backward for you to ensure you get what you want. Or, in the famous words of the late Zig Ziglar: "You can have everything in life you want if you will just help enough other people get what they want."[3]

CHAPTER 4

Partners versus Sellers

I'm looking for people who are looking for me.

—SEAN LANGSTON

IN THE WEEDS

In Matthew 13:24–30, Jesus shares a parable about the wheat and the weeds. A farmer sows seeds of wheat in his field, but in the night, an enemy sows thistles among the wheat crop. "When the crop began to grow, the thistles grew too."[1] One worker is worried the thistles will choke the wheat and asks if he should pull them. The farmer advises against this as this would uproot the good wheat. Instead, wait until harvest to sort out.

The parable illustrates the good and the bad can coexist and grow together. The ultimate separation will occur at the end of time. It teaches patience and caution, but it also suggests we must not make hasty judgments.

This verse speaks of the true meaning of a business partner. Finding the right partner takes time and patience. It took dozens of failed relationships for me to finally find my wife, but it was worth it! And in the beginning of my investing career, it took hundreds of sellers to finally find one who was open to my creative offer. As time passed and my patience grew, that ratio became closer to one out of a hundred sellers.

Still, worth it!

PEOPLE: THE TRUE ASSET

The real estate business is a people business, and people have problems. This business is about helping people and solving problems. It's never about the house. Our business revolves around people's hardship. We wouldn't be in business if there weren't hardships. People will still have problems—with or without us. We didn't create this hardship. Rather, our job is to resolve their pain. We learn about their situation and see if we can help them find a way out.

The mission of my investment company is to *help sellers out, help buyers in.* I aim to help sellers *out* of a sticky situation and help buyers *into* a home of their own. I seek to help as many people as possible. But if I am to establish a long-term relationship, it can only succeed if it's a mutual partnership. After all, I'm going to be in a relationship with these people for years!

So, I must ask myself: *Is this a person I want to partner with for the next three, five, or potentially twenty years?* If my answer is no, we don't do business. As entrepreneurs, you and I have the ability to select who we do business with.

Conversely, in corporate America, we have to take on any customer willing to pay for the product or service.

Our job is to learn about the seller and their situation. What is their situation? What happened in their life that they now need to sell their property? This can be a sensitive subject. However, when you show up as someone who can help, you don't have to worry about bringing up sensitive information.[2]

Most people will not readily share their personal information. At least, not at first. This takes time. Trust isn't built in a single conversation. In my experience, the timeline from first contact to signing a contract to closing can be anywhere from three months to twenty-four months! I counted the number of seller touchpoints from my previously closed deals and found that it took an average of twenty-seven text messages, thirteen emails, seven voice messages, and two video conference calls. Does that sound like a lot? It is.

Still… worth it!

If you always look for a solution to seemingly unsolvable problems, you'll be the last one standing when it's time to cash in on the deal.[3] The better you can position yourself as the answer to their problem, the more quickly they will trust you. Trust isn't given, it's earned!

BUT AREN'T YOU TAKING ADVANTAGE OF PEOPLE?

People think that, as real estate investors, we're asking sellers for all of their equity in their home. I disagree. I ask them what they want for their house. If I can give them their asking price, we make the deal. If not, I will tell them what I could pay. If they accept, we move forward. Whether I accept their price and my terms or they accept my price and their terms, two people have made an agreement. If one person makes an offer and the other accepts, then there's no dilemma.

Nevertheless, this stereotype of twisting grandma's arm persists. I've experienced this stigma from thousands of sellers over the years. And there are plenty of investors who continue to operate in this way. The market shows evidence of this. Below are just a handful of the derogatory responses I receive on a weekly basis from my social media advertising.

"Scam!"

"Vultures!"

"Con artist."

"How do you live with yourself?"

"Just send me an offer. Then, we'll talk."

Ouch! Now, I know they're not attacking me. Rather, they're responding to the thistles that have already pricked them and tried to choke them out. They're simply projecting their past experiences of other investors onto you and me. There's no need to engage them and explain how we're different. As you learned in chapter three, these are the 99 percent. Let them continue to graze with the rest of the flock.

This business is for-profit. We're not running a charity. There's no need to hide what we're doing. Just because I'm a Christian doesn't mean I'm a nonprofit organization. God won't be offended if you make a profit. My investor friend, Eric Lyman, says, "If we merely send them an offer, we're ultimately running a free consulting business." Without money, the mission of *helping sellers out* becomes choked out.

For-profit doesn't mean your business can't also lean on a *for-faith* framework.

CIRCUMSTANCE VERSUS CITY

So, where should we invest? Short answer: where no one else is. I'm not interested in a particular city. I don't invest in a *market.* Instead, I invest in a seller's *circumstance.* The circumstances you and I should be listening for are:

- The sellers do not have a large amount of equity in their property.
    - The mortgage loan balance is at or near market value.
- They do not need all their cash upfront to purchase another property.
    - Most have already moved out and are either renting or living with family.
- They are realistic about the property value.
- They do not want to pay a real estate agent or closing costs nor deal with flakey buyers.
    - They might have already listed it on the market with no success.
- They are looking for a hassle-free sale.

- Their property needs work, and they don't want to make the improvements.
- They are emotionally "done" with the property.
- They have a tenant living there who is not paying the rent.
  - These are my favorite because I sweeten the deal by offering to remove their tenant for them.

So, regardless of what city the seller resides in, you and I are able to help them out. The more boxes we can check off from the above list, the better we can help them, whether they live in a population of three hundred, three thousand, or thirty thousand. Rural America is where all my deals have come from because there is not a lot of cash buyers or investors/house-flippers.

But some investors make it only about the money at the mercy of people. This is a slippery slope where trust isn't established and greed becomes the driving force.

GREED

This industry is full of greed. And left unchecked, that greed can consume any investor. That's why we need to lean on God to check us. We aren't disciplined enough to set up our own checks and balances. God wants each one of us to succeed. He just wants us to include Him in the process and not be greedy.

The numbers are the first thing we look at when analyzing a deal. If the numbers don't make sense, no deal! But, as crucial as the financials are, if the people involved don't make sense—no deal!

Before Christ, I would see how much I could squeeze the seller to get what I wanted. On my first creative finance deal, I promised to give the seller a $10,000 down payment. One week prior to closing, I couldn't come up with the money. Instead of informing the seller immediately, I waited until the last minute to confess. On closing day, I informed him I could only give him $5,000. This was obviously a property over people move that I must now live with.

On my second creative finance deal, I agreed to pay the seller's mortgage payments for her. Within a few months, my tenant trashed the place, and the city condemned the property. With the property now uninhabitable, I stopped paying the seller's mortgage for eight months, and the house was going into foreclosure for nonpayment. On one of my wholesale deals, I signed a contract knowing full well I couldn't close because there were no investors willing to buy. I was the enemy sowing bad seeds in sellers' fields. These behaviors were clearly misaligned to that of a good partner.

That's when my investor friend, Benji, reminded me:

A good name is more valuable than riches. We must hold on to our integrity, tell the truth, and never put money above the moral. What's the point of gaining the whole world and forfeiting your soul? Proverbs 21:2 says *we can justify our every deed, but God looks at our motives.* If you want to be first, you will be last.

This was the exact reminder I needed. I made a vow to never squeeze another seller out of the money I promised. I found another tenant who was willing to repair the condemned property if I caught up with the mortgage payments, and I never enter into a contract if I don't fully believe I can close. God taught me if a good partner is what I'm seeking, then I must *become* the partner with whom I seek.

As my property portfolio grew from my neighborhood, to my city, to my state, to a nationwide reach, a level of anonymity grew. I never physically meet the seller in person, nor do I physically step into the property. That said, I must constantly remind myself there is a human on the other side of the phone who needs help.

Nowadays, every morning at 7:45 a.m. before I begin my work, I have an alarm on my phone that says: *How would I behave if God was my business partner?* This question is a reminder that I'm doing business with His people, and His people need love and respect.

Years ago, I purchased a property in Mississippi where I promised to pay the seller a monthly payment for five years. After eighteen months, I was notified the seller passed away. *Woohoo! A free house!* I thought. Eight months later, I received a call from the seller's heir asking how much I owed. I instructed him to contact a probate attorney, and within a short time, I began making payments to his heir.

Not long afterward, the heir fell upon hard times and needed money. He asked if I'd just pay him the full balance. "I can, but only at a deep discount," I explained. We agreed on a payoff amount that worked for both of us. The next morning, as I was typing up the new agreement, my phone alarm went off: *How would I behave if God was my business partner?*

Oof! I immediately called the heir.

"Are you sure you want to do this? After all, you stand to make more money if we continue the monthly payment arrangement," I pleaded.

"You're right. Let's keep the agreement as is," he confirmed.

The heir was so pleased with my honesty that we're now doing a similar type of creative finance arrangement for another property he owns. God helped me remove the thistles in my behavior before they had a chance to choke the good seed.

My accountability partner, Jason Pucel, leads a ministry called Grace by the Drop. In his YouTube video, Jason noted, "It always comes at a price when we don't consult God on our business endeavors. God won't bless compromised negotiations, although He'll help you get out of them."[4] God speaks to people through His people. Accountability is the annoying little secret of success. And the kingdom advances through His relationships.[5]

So, what does a good partnership look like? A bad partnership? How would you know if the partnership is so ugly you should run for the hills?

PARTNERSHIPS: THE GOOD, THE BAD, AND THE UGLY

The following stories are real-life examples of what a partnership *is* and what a partnership is *not*.

THE GOOD: KANSAS KEEPER

A seller in Kansas had already moved out of state, and her ex's niece was living there paying the mortgage. She had tried to list the property, but it needed too much repair. The seller was communicative, open, and honest. She'd responded to my social media ad, completed a property intake form, scheduled a phone consultation, answered my phone call at the appointment time, understood my offer, and agreed to move forward. She was the 1 percent I'd been praying for.

We would have closed that same week, except we needed to get her ex's niece out. Within a few short weeks after she moved out, I found my tenant. The seller was so pleased she recommended me to a friend, and we closed on her friend's property two months later.

THE BAD: WAYWARD IN WEST VIRGINIA

I have a folder of "Dead Deals" stored on my computer. I aim to close every deal that comes my way. But sometimes, it's out of my control. These deals weren't dead on arrival because the numbers didn't work or the property needed too much in repairs. No. Each deal had the potential to be profitable.

These deals died because achieving a win-win with the seller was nearly impossible. The sellers were not open, honest, or communicative. With each one, I agreed to the seller's purchase price. We worked out an agreeable closing date and negotiated a reasonable monthly payment. I took care of everything: paying closing costs, coordinating with attorneys, title companies, and locksmiths, and turning on utilities. Unfortunately, these sellers just didn't want to sell, even after we had a signed contract.

I could technically sue the seller for specific performance. The seller did not *perform* what they *specifically* agreed to do—sell me their house. But I found it's not worth chasing dead deals. By the time I'd hire an attorney, file a notice of memorandum with the county clerk to cloud the title, and engage in months of frivolous lawsuits, what would I have really gained? The fact remained *the seller didn't want to do business with me.* It's like forcing someone to marry me on the first date after they've clearly expressed a disinterest! That's not how the dating world works, and it's not how the real estate world works either.

 A seller in West Virginia inherited a property she didn't want and was ready to sell. "I want to be done, done, *done* with this property!" she explained. We agreed on $5,000 cash. The relationship started out great. She completed my property intake form, scheduled a phone call, and actually called *me* at the scheduled time of the appointment. Our next step was to perform a video walk-through the following week.

This is where the deal began to fall apart. We had to reschedule seven different times because of other, more pressing matters. Then, she ghosted me. However, I wasn't giving up that easily. My automated follow-up system continued to nurture her each month with soft, casual check-ins—still no response. After nine months, she finally called me back.

"I'm ready to sell."

"Oh. Hi. I remember you."

"Yes. Sorry. I've been really busy."

"I understand. How about I send you a lock box to put on the front door? That way, I can hire an inspector and photographer. You don't have to worry about a thing."

"That'd be great!"

I mailed the lockbox. She confirmed it had arrived. Then came more excuses. "Oh. I'm sick... my brother had emergency surgery... my daughter had a thing come up... I'm out of town... I'm working on a big project right now..."

Finally, I'd had enough. I removed her from my automated follow-up system—I was done, done, *done*! Clearly, she was part of the 99 percent. Even *if* she was ever ready to sell, it wouldn't be to me. I'd lost interest. I was done chasing this dead deal. I was done trying to force her to marry me after she told me (indirectly) she had no interest on our first date.

One of my colleagues had a similar situation with a seller in North Carolina. What should have taken two weeks took over twelve months! Luckily, he ended up closing his deal. He found out on the day of closing the seller was a cocaine addict. The attorney said he could hear the seller snorting cocaine in the bathroom! Certainly not partner material.

THE UGLY: LOUISIANA LIAR

I'd almost closed on a property in Louisiana about an hour east of Shreveport.

I was willing to accept the termites, the structural damage, and the undesirable location. What I couldn't accept was the seller's lies. After seven months and seventeen conversations with the seller, we signed a contract using a sandwich lease option (see chapter nine). The seller didn't like the idea of a stranger (me) owning the home while the mortgage remained in his name. So, we agreed he would still own the property, and I would lease it from him with the intent to purchase it outright within a few years.

My attorney conducted a title search and discovered that several liens—a hospital bill lien, a mechanic's lien, and a property tax lien—had been placed on the property, thus clouding the title. Each lien would have to be paid to transfer a clear title down the road. Such a discovery would potentially be a deal breaker… except the total amount needed to clear these liens, including attorney's fees, was $1,000. I offered to pay each lien and explained to the seller this amount would be deducted from the amount he'd receive at closing.

"Woah. Slow your roll! I have no knowledge of any of these liens that your so-called attorney found. You need to pay me what you promised."

"Mr. Seller, these are your liens. You want me to take a loss for something I had no control over?"

"I don't care what your so-called attorney found. If you're not going to pay me what you promised, the deal is off!"

I still wanted the deal—liens and all. I had already found my tenant-buyer. Their down payment would have been three times more than my cost to acquire the deal.

"I'm willing to pay each lien *and* still give you *all* the money we originally agreed to."

Still, as much as I tried, I couldn't get him to understand that we had to have an official closing. He thought by signing our contract, I was going to pay six months of his late mortgage payments before we even officially closed our deal with an attorney.

Ninety-nine!

Two months after we parted ways, I received a call from the fraud department of a large insurance company.

"Do you own this property?" the investigator asked.

"No. I tried to buy it, but the seller backed out. How did my name come up anyway?" I answered nervously.

"We show that you turned on the utilities recently. We're just trying to get in touch with the owner because he filed a claim for damages. But our site inspection proved the damages were preexisting. We have reason to believe this is a fraudulent claim," he explained.

If I had moved forward with this, who knows how many more liens or fraudulent insurance claims the seller would have placed on the property? As of this writing, the seller still hasn't sold, and the bank is getting ready to foreclose. This behavior is certainly not a characteristic of a trustworthy partner. I didn't want to deal with this seller for another five years or even another five minutes!

Strike one: no trust.

Strike two: no communication.

Strike three: no accountability.

Three strikes… you're out!

You won't always know immediately if your seller will be a good partner after the first phone call. Luckily, most of creative financing arrangements we'll discuss in chapter nine take several months to complete and require multiple touch points between the time of initial contact to signed contract to close. This lag in time allows you to gauge the quality of their character and helps you understand if you're seller is a true partner.

RELATIONSHIPS: THE TRUE ASSET

Property is the asset: it paves the path to passive income and financial freedom.

A property appreciates over time and pays dividends in the form of monthly cash flow, tax write-offs, and principal pay down. It appreciates 3 to 7 percent every year, depending on the location, the market cycle, and how we nurture and maintain the property.

The same is true about people in our property. If we nurture the relationships with our people, we gain even greater forms of appreciation—both tangible and intangible—such as goodwill, amicable negotiations, greater adherence to the contract, raving reviews, referrals, and reciprocated respect.

The only real capital we have ownership of in this world is our *relationships*. Once I began treating the relationship with my sellers as a partnership, the transactions flowed much more smoothly. We're not only investing in real *property*. We're also investing in real *people*.

The purpose of this book is to plant a stronger wheat crop of investors who refuse to be choked out by the thistles.

Real estate investing will provide passive profits that can fertilize your future fields of freedom. That's why I started. And I so want this for you too. But even more importantly, I want you to learn how to buy investment properties without selling *your soul*!

We do this by treating our sellers as partners versus adversaries. Aim to work with partners and watch your portfolio prosper. Remember, it's never about the house.

CHAPTER 5

Partners versus Tenant-Buyers

You can succeed best and quickest by helping others to succeed.[1]

—NAPOLEON HILL

Just as we've learned to only work with sellers who want to work with us, the same holds true for our tenant-buyers (i.e., renters who intend to buy the property). Properties don't pay us; people do. Since we're going to be in a relationship with our tenant-buyer for years, it's crucial we treat them as partners. Remember, property is merely the vehicle. *People* are the engine.

THE BARREN FIG TREE

In Luke 13:6–9, Jesus provides an illustration of a barren fig tree that hasn't produced fruit for three years. The farmer instructed his gardener to cut it down. "Why bother with it any longer? It's taking up space we can use for something else,"[2] the farmer concluded. "Give it one more chance. Leave it for another year, and I will give it special attention and plenty of fertilizer. If we get figs next year, fine. If not, I'll cut it down," explained the gardener.[3] The vineyard owner grants the tree another year of life.

God expects His people to bear fruit, but it requires time and patience. God is patient and gives us time to change our lives and bear good spiritual fruit. We can help our tenants-buyers into a home they never thought possible if we can just be patient and offer a little more time.

INVEST IN PEOPLE WHO INVEST IN PROPERTY

People who cannot obtain traditional bank financing look to rent-to-own as a solution. These *tenant-buyers* typically have prior blemishes on their credit, their amount of debt relative to their income may be too high, or they are self-employed and do not have the steady stream of income that mortgage lenders require. In short, they are *unbankable.*

They may have given up on the idea of homeownership. But, as investors, you and I can offer these people a chance to establish stronger roots in a better financial future. They lease your property with the intent to purchase it once they improve their situation. Since you are accepting a risk that a bank is not, your tenant-buyer is willing to pay a premium because they understand they'll eventually own the home versus throwing away money in rent. But just like the barren fig tree, it takes time and patience to bear fruit.

Our property is fixed; it's stagnant. People, on the other hand, are dynamic and ever-changing. Most tenant-buyers who dream of owning a home are ready to commit to changing their circumstances. They just need someone like you and me to give them the chance that banks won't.

Remember, properties don't pay us; people do. People are the fruit; the property is merely the tree. Just like the fig tree, it takes time, patience, and proper care to equip these tenant-buyers to become loan-ready. Since this partnership could potentially last several years, it's crucial we only invest in the people who are going to invest in *their* property, even while the property is still under your legal control.

WORK FOR EQUITY PROGRAM

Some of the properties you'll acquire have a large amount of deferred maintenance. The seller has basically let the house go because they do not have the money or the time to fix it. Other sellers are emotionally disconnected from the property and have given up.

I invest nationwide and have no interest in finding local contractors in small-town USA to perform repairs. That is the main reason you should consider offering the property as a rent to own: tenant-buyers are responsible for all maintenance, upkeep, and repairs (i.e., you're off the hook for late night calls, clogged toilets, or leaky roofs).

So, aim for a client who can make repairs if the property needs work. Most tenant-buyers are excited to fix up the property in any way they like to make the house their home. Any repairs they perform that increase the value of the property are deducted from their purchase price.

You sell the property to tenant-buyer as-is—at full market price. *Why would anyone buy a run-down house at full market price*, you ask? Great question. Most won't! Those with vision, however, are incentivized because they see how much they can reduce their purchase price by using their own sweat-equity, or what Ron LeGrand calls the "Work for Equity Program."

Any improvements the tenant-buyer performs that increase the value of the property are credited toward the purchase price after pictures, invoices, and receipts are submitted. If they spend $2,500 on flooring, the purchase price is reduced by $2,500. If they replace the roof, A/C, water heater, counters, etc., their purchase price is reduced dollar for dollar.

The tenant-buyer who is willing to put in their own money and sweat into repairing a property that will eventually be theirs is more committed and willing to take the necessary steps to not only repair the property but also repair their credit so they can purchase the property and call it their own. Like the fig tree, they just need time and patience.

"RENT-TO-OWN IS A SCAM!"

Outsiders looking in may think we're taking advantage of these tenant-buyers, similar to how sellers view investors: scam artists! And just like sellers, the market shows evidence of this stigma:

"Scam!"

"Beware!"

"Ripoff!"

"Fake news!"

I receive these common responses on a weekly basis from my rent-to-own advertising. I've seen scam artists take my advertisement and repost it on their platform, asking prospects to "look in the windows and then send $500 to see inside!" My heart goes out to anyone who has been a victim of such heists.

You squash the scam concept and establish credibility by explaining that you'll close the transaction with a local real estate attorney who will record the deal with the county clerk. The tenant-buyer will not wire you the down payment. Rather, they'll send the down payment and first month's payment to the attorney's office—making it more official.

You also express full transparency from the start. Your ad clearly states the purchase price, the monthly payment, and the repairs needed, as well as the terms of the rent-to-own agreement. If the tenant-buyer accepts, you move forward. There's no coercion or arm wrestling. Two people have made an agreement. If one person makes an offer and the other accepts, then there's no dilemma—just like with sellers.

And just like sellers, we look at each tenant-buyer's specific circumstance instead of only looking at our dollar signs and bottom lines.

CIRCUMSTANCE VERSUS CREDIT SCORE

We seek to help as many people as possible. After all, they are all God's people. You'll run a credit check and background check—but you're not so concerned about credit score. You've already established that your audience may not have the best credit situation, but they desire to improve their score and are willing to take the necessary steps to raise it. If you are to establish a partnership with them, you must understand not only how they manage debt (i.e., FICO credit score) but also how they manage their money *and* their morals, or what I will call their FICO *debit* score.

FICO debit score factors include:

F—Financial:
- 10–20 percent down payment
- Gross monthly income = three times the monthly rent
- Twelve months of steady, verifiable income
- On time payment history

I—Intelligence:
- Emotional IQ
- Honesty
- Open and communicative
- Respectful
- Competency in understanding the terms of the agreement

C—Credit/Criminal:
- 600-plus credit score
- No repossessions
- No bankruptcies
- No felonies

- No evictions
- Ready to enroll in a credit repair program

O—Ownership:
- How much ownership do they take regarding their past?
- Do they carry a "woe is me" or entitled attitude?
- What's their level of commitment to owning a home? How excited are they about the opportunity?
- Do they already think, speak, and act like an owner, or are they simply rushing to get into a place because of their current circumstances?

My friend, Jim Horn, says he doesn't always accept the tenant-buyer with the highest down payment—even though that'd be the most profitable. But would it? It just depends on how you define profit. If you're defining profit merely as how much down payment you receive without considering the relationship or any of the other factors described above, tread lightly. The hidden costs of accepting a potential quack far outweigh a large down payment!

Of all the FICO debit score criteria described above, Jim places the most weight on: How excited is the tenant-buyer about the opportunity to get into their very own home? This is the client who will take the best care of the property because they know it will be *theirs*. They will gladly enroll in—and maintain good standing in—the credit repair program, they will pay on time and in full without ever being asked, and they will make improvements to the property that increase its value. They understand they are investing in their financial future.

That's the type of partner you want to work with every time.

THE QUALIFIED, THE QUIRKY, AND THE QUACK

As much as we like to think we are a good judge of character, you can only gauge so much from what tenant-buyers look like on paper and a few telephone conversations. You lose that richness of communication that comes with face-to-face interaction. People's true character becomes more apparent when their back is against the wall (i.e., they can't pay the monthly payment and you can't get a hold of them).

Obviously, you'll aim to locate the qualified tenant-buyer using the criteria explained earlier in this chapter. However, there are circumstances beyond your ability to judge a person's character that factor in. You aren't always able to find your qualified tenant-buyer and may end up with someone who may be quirkier—or possibly even a quack!

Several factors that may limit you from locating your qualified tenant-buyer include:

- Condition of the property
    - Seller has deferred too much maintenance
- Location of the property
    - Bad area of town
- Population
    - Small town; fewer tenant-buyers
- Demographic
    - Rural America doesn't always have a high socioeconomic class; expecting a 10–20 percent down payment is not feasible.
- Time and patience
    - Several months may have passed, and you've agreed to pay the seller's mortgage to avoid foreclosure.

Your monthly *out-go* is greater than your incoming *cash flow.*

You can certainly mitigate these risks by choosing to invest *only* in rent-ready properties located in the upper end of large metro areas. But, just like the fig tree, that strategy will require more time and patience to locate these unicorn properties.

Leverage both the credit score and debit score to understand your tenant-buyer's situation. But also factor in the location, population, and proper risk mitigation to land your qualified client in the sea of quirkies and quacks.

Let's now explore some of the first steps you'll need to land that qualified partner.

YOU HAVE A SIGNED CONTRACT WITH THE SELLER. NOW WHAT?

Once you and the seller have signed the contract, you inform them you'll begin marketing the property to attract your tenant-buyer—even though you don't own the property yet. The signed purchase contract gives you equitable interest in the property, which offers you the right to market it. Be sure to let the seller know they may begin to see their property on the market as a rent-to-own. It's far better they understand this before they find out for themselves.

Prior to closing, you mail the seller a lock box to place on the front door so you can show the property to your tenant-buyer prospects. If you're not comfortable with this approach, you can hire a local real estate agent to help you.

Once you've purchased the property and the seller has moved out, you begin scheduling showings for your qualified candidates. Every prospect will want to see inside, naturally. Unfortunately, 90 percent of these interested prospects will not meet the FICO debit requirements described above. Setting up an automated screening system allows the qualified partners to naturally rise above and disqualify the quirkies and the quacks.

Only those who complete a questionnaire, schedule a phone call, show up for the phone call, and meet most—if not all—of your FICO requirements are able to view inside. That way, you don't have to worry about anyone having access to your property who would cause damage, run off with the key, or squat in your property.

BUT WHAT IF THE TENANT BUYER DEFAULTS?

Sadly, more than 40 percent of my tenant-buyers haven't worked out. This number may seem high. But keep in mind we're working with people that banks won't. It's logical that not everyone is going to work out. But if their FICO debit score checks out, I believe everyone deserves a second chance. There are good people who've been through bad experiences.

If they default for nonpayment, you must evict them, and the contract you recorded at the county clerk must be nullified. If they willingly back out because of a personal life event, you cancel the contract and offer to be a good reference for their next home. In either case, they understand their down payment was nonrefundable. If they damage the property, you place it back on the market as a handyperson's special and get another nonrefundable down payment from a new tenant-buyer.

Many of my best tenant-buyers have come on the second time around, after I've had a poor experience with the first. Just like the fig tree, it takes time, patience, and proper nurturing.

The following are a handful of personal experiences I encountered in my first few years of investing. Hopefully, these real-life examples help you more clearly understand what a partnership *is* and what it is *not*.

CASE STUDY: THE QUALIFIED, THE QUIRKY, AND THE QUACK

THE QUALIFIED—NEW YORK NEWCOMER

A couple who was new to the area took an interest in one of my fixer-uppers in New York.

They had vision and saw past the property's current condition. They were forthcoming about their past and didn't try to hide anything. What most impressed me was they actually *read* the entire contract and asked clarifying questions. They thought, spoke, and acted like owners.

They remained enrolled in the credit repair program for the full term. They had the necessary construction experience to perform the property improvements themselves. The after pictures they sent were immaculate! If they knew they were going to pay late, they would notify me well in advance.

I couldn't have asked for a better partner!

THE QUIRKY: VIRGINIA VAGABOND

I agreed to help the seller remove her nonpaying tenant, which ended up taking several months.

A young man expressed a strong interest in the property on the very first day, but I told him to hang tight while I got the seller's tenant out. His FICO debit score didn't rank him as qualified, maybe just a little quirky.

He'd been living with his father temporarily but also with his girlfriend and even with his other friends—I never got the full story. He was a fireman and was about to get married. He dreamed of owning a home for his future family.

He paid each payment during the first few months but was notoriously late. On month five, I could no longer reach him. It was radio silence. I contacted his father, who promised he'd have my tenant call me. Three days later, I texted his father to follow up and received an automated text back stating the father had blocked my number.

The tenant finally called me and shared this story:

"I just got out of jail. My girlfriend made up a story that I abused her. She left me, and I lost my job because of it. I assure you that you'll be paid in full next week. I'm going to sell my car today."

"But if you sell your car, how are you going to get to your job?" I inquired.

"I'll figure it out," he assured me.

"Okay, call me tomorrow after you sell your car. If I don't hear from you, I am filing an eviction."

Next day: no call, no text, no surprise!

I filed for eviction and had a new tenant-buyer backfilled within six weeks. After paying over $1,000 to evict him and change the locks, this Virginia vagabond had the nerve to reach out six months later, asking if he could rent the place again.

Umm… no!

THE QUACK: NORTH CAROLINA NONVERBAL

One of the most dilapidated homes I've ever purchased was a duplex in North Carolina. No way would I ever find a buyer for this property in the winter season! In a desperate attempt to get a warm body, I selected a family who talked a big game: They knew how to handle any construction project and were reliable and trustworthy.

Within the first month, they explained how someone came and *removed* the outdoor air conditioning unit. They insisted I give them credit for having to install a new one.

They told me about all the improvements they'd made to the property, yet they never sent me one picture, receipt, or invoice. They explained how the property needed foundation work and a new well (even though I knew it did not). They'd changed jobs but never provided me with their new employer contact information.

About four months in, they stopped paying and stopped answering my calls and texts. I called their old employer, who'd said they'd never given him two weeks' notice. They simply stopped showing up for work. It's interesting how quickly a quirky can turn quack!

I emailed them the notice to vacate and indicated that an eviction would appear on their record, which finally elicited a response:

"We've already moved out because the rodents, bats, and flea infestation was so bad."

What? I had no idea. This family had been living in this circumstance for almost four months. Gross!

It took another forty-five days and screening through sixty-seven different tenant-buyer prospects to finally find someone with the vision to look past the property imperfections. It just proves there is a buyer for every property.

PATIENT AND PRACTICAL

I share these stories not to scare you but to help you avoid some of the mistakes I made when I first began investing. You don't need a highlight reel showcasing all my trophies. That wouldn't serve you. I'd rather be transparent and show you my battle scars so you can take a shorter path to finding your perfect partner.

I spoke with Pastor David Brockhouse about my shortcomings as a landlord-partner. He related his pastoral work to that of a landlord by saying, "I lord over people at the church, but I don't lord over their lives—that job is already taken." His advice when dealing with troublesome tenants is to judge or attack the performance, not the person. Excellent advice: We are responsible to lord over the property—*not* the people!

In another discussion with Pastor Sean Metcalf, he reminded me that God's suffering is long. But He wants us to learn from our suffering. If we never uphold our word (of the partnership) with our tenant-buyers, how would they believe that we uphold our word to Christ?

In the beginning, I would purchase any property where the seller was open to creative financing. Now, I'm more selective. I would also partner with any tenant-buyer who said they could fix the property and had a down payment. Now, I'm more deliberate. You may be anxious to purchase and lease the first house that comes along. You want your financial tree to bear fruit. But learn from my mistakes and don't rush it. One of the fruits of the spirit discussed in the book of Galatians is patience. At times we need to be patient like the gardener and give it one more chance. Other times, we must be practical like the farmer and cut it down by saying "No!" to a property or to a tenant-buyer, which is the subject of the next chapter: Evictions.

CHAPTER 6

Evictions

We are only tenants, and shortly the great Landlord will give us notice that our lease has expired.[1]

—JOSEPH JEFFERSON

INTIMATELY ENGAGED

The tenant/landlord relationship is like no other business transaction. It is the most interesting and unique exchange form of commerce in the world today. In any other business exchange, if you don't pay, the service ends. When you don't pay your phone bill, the company shuts off your service. If your employer doesn't pay you for the work you've completed, you quit! Yet, when a tenant decides not to pay rent, they continue to receive service (i.e., they continue living in the property). Sure, the landlord files an eviction and regains access to the property—but only after three weeks or three months, depending on the state, the court, the judge, and the tenant's plea.

As real estate investors, our job is to solve other people's problems. That's what we get paid for. But we often become so filled with greed that we take the human aspect out of the equation. Or worse, we extend so much empathy to the point at which someone else's problem becomes ours! Therefore, we must establish the right boundary line of when to let it go and when to say, "No!" If you have difficulty setting limits, you may be the one who has the boundary problem; however, those who don't respect other's limits also have boundary problems.[2]

BREAKING BOUNDARIES

In Matthew 18:23–34, Jesus shares a parable about forgiveness. A king called in one of his debtors who owed a large amount of money. The debtor fell at the king's feet and pleaded, "Be patient with me, and I will pay it."[3] The king felt pity for this man and forgave his entire debt. Shortly after leaving the king, the man went to one of his debtors, who owed him a much smaller amount of money, choked him, and demanded immediate payment. The king discovered what this man had done and had him tortured until he paid the king back every last penny!

"Here I forgave you all that tremendous debt, just because you asked me to—shouldn't you have mercy on others, just as I had mercy on you?"[4]

Yet, in Matthew 21: 33–41, Jesus shares another parable about when a boundary line must be enforced.

A landowner leased his grape vineyard to others on a sharecropping basis. The workers became greedy and attempted to take the proceeds for themselves by stoning and killing any of the landowner's agents who came to collect the harvest. Although Jesus was indicating that the Pharisees were the wicked servants in the story, it also applies to your tenants who feel they do not need to pay rent. What will the landowner do to the servants when he returns? "He will… lease the vineyard to others who will pay him promptly."[5]

HURT VERSUS HARM

Every decision has a consequence. My lower back has become the recipient of all my poor decisions made in my youth—falling off ladders, failing to lift heavy objects with my legs, cliff jumping, and poor posture—all of which caused harm to my body, especially to my lower back. I was on pain meds for a few years, which stopped the *hurt*—but these meds were causing me *harm* in other ways: reduced sex drive and lack of focus.

I eventually had two surgeries, which provided some long-term relief. The physical hurt caused by the surgery was excruciating—but in the long run, it did not harm me. The pain during recovery was exacerbated because I refused to take any more pain meds. I quit cold turkey. I finally realized no magic pill or surgery was going to relieve my hurt. If I want to stay out of harm's way, I must use a standing desk, move more, lose weight, and adjust my exercise regimen; basically, all the things I knew I was supposed to do, but have chosen not to do up to that point because it caused temporary hurt. Yet, this short-term hurt of diet and exercise hasn't caused any long-term harm.

EVICTIONS HURT

Many people I've met tell me they'd never invest in property because they don't want to deal with tenants. They've heard too many horror stories of their family's or friend's experiences. Their perceived risk of loss outweighs the reward of financial and time freedom.

Evictions are one of the hardest things we do as investors. It's the end of a partnership, a reflection of us failing to select the right partner for this long-term relationship. Not only does it hurt us as investors to evict, it hurts our tenants even more. However, it's certainly not harming them. Enforcing this boundary of *no pay—no stay* signals they can no longer play the victim role. Will they gain this understanding during the process? Probably not. In fairness, I rarely learn what God is teaching me in that moment when I'm down in the dumps!

Nevertheless, we can't grow for others, nor can we eat for another person. God does not enable irresponsible behavior. Throughout the scriptures, people are reminded of their choices and asked to take responsibility for them:

"Hunger is good—if it makes you work to satisfy it."[6]

"Each of us must bear some faults and burdens of his own."[7]

"He who does not work shall not eat."[8]

When I first began investing, I did so without God. I'd offer too much truth and not enough grace. As I allowed God to enter into my business, I landed on the extreme opposite end:

too much grace and no truth. I'd feel guilty for charging late fees and often give in to the tenants' sob stories.

My business, which was supposed to be providing financial freedom, quickly turned into a nonprofit organization!

I was waving late fees, accepting partial payments, and letting a month's payment slide—essentially carrying other people's load. However, as I've matured in both my faith and my business, I no longer allow others to take advantage of me or feel guilt for it.

We must help our fellow brothers and sisters—of course! But not to the point of hurting our ability to support our own families. We must help those in need—obviously. But not if it harms us by crossing our own boundary line. There's a time for bearing each other's burdens. There's also a time when each of us must carry our own load.

I now use a three-strikes rule, and I suggest you do the same. After three late payments, it's time to go. The more volatile the payment cycle, the more crucial the need to communicate becomes. If the tenant knows they're going to be late, and they don't tell you, that's a red flag. If you have to chase the tenant down, they are not a partner worth keeping. My coach and mentor, John Burley, told me that "after twenty days of being late, there's no catching up. We've tried to work with you each step, and you haven't done your part." If they've reached the point of being forcibly removed, they've got bigger problems than just paying you. Yes, they need help. But no, you do not need to carry their load! Their problem doesn't need to be your problem any longer than necessary.

I began to wonder, *Am I way off in my thinking here? How do others see this sore subject?* I began asking other investors and even spoke with a couple of pastors on this topic of evictions.

TWO VIEWS, SAME POINT

A PASTOR'S PERSPECTIVE

Pastor Justin Weaver specializes in youth ministry but is also a part-time real estate investor focusing on foreclosures. He's not afraid to do what is necessary to remove a tenant who hasn't paid their mortgage in months. Justin leans on 2 Thessalonians 3:10, which says if anyone is not willing to work, let him not eat. He says, "Inequality is baked into the way God made the world. It is His way of producing bounty. Property ownership is a privilege for kingdom Christians, not a right. Hold lightly so as not to be choked by thorns and thistles."

This resonated well with me because I had three tenants where I was offering too much grace and not enough truth. The truth was they were taking advantage of me. I was carrying their load. Their thistles (inability to pay) became piercing thorns in my ability to offer bounty to other tenants who were ready and willing to pay.

In an interview with my pastor, Ed Newton, I explained this idea of cash for keys, where I offered to pay the tenant to move out in exchange for the keys to the house. Ultimately, I forfeit the money they owe me and give them even more money if they'll just leave. That way, they don't have an eviction charge on their record, and I regain control of the house.

"And where does this cash come from?" Ed asked.

"From other tenants who pay on time," I said.

"Exactly! You're giving away your profit margin. So, not collecting the rent from this tenant prevents you from being charitable in other areas! You must get them out to be a blessing for others. You can't be a blessing to others who *can* pay, nor give the tithes you normally would to your community, if this nonperforming tenant stays! Let them know, 'You're making me be a blessing to you *only*. What about the four other people that I was going to bless this month?' You're only able to do cash for keys because others are abiding by the contract and doing what they said they're going to do," he shared. Preach, pastor!

I recently joined Faith Driven Entrepreneurs to connect with other faith-based business owners. We were talking about how we handle failures and losses. My friend, Claudette, shared, "In the past, it used to really bother me when I suffered a loss in my business. Nowadays, I learned to view these losses simply as tithes to the business." Woah! This had me thinking: *I cheerfully give to the church and the community to help bless other people, yet I'm unwilling to let one late payment slide. What if my blessing this month was to waive this late fee one time and attribute it as a tithe to my business?*

A PROFESSIONAL POINT OF VIEW

As business owners, we all like to think we are a good judge of character. We think we're so good at hiring. We tell ourselves, "I just feel right about this person. They've got a great heart." The truth is: we suck at hiring. Businessman and author Gary Vaynerchuk shares, "I've got really good hiring advice: learn to fire fast."[9] A criminal and credit background check acts as the initial interview in selecting the right tenant. But you can only learn so much about a person from how they appear on paper. You won't really know their character until they owe you money and are avoiding your phone calls.

After interviewing pastors and preachers, I was curious to see how other active real estate investors handle their own evictions. My friend and mentor, Blair Halver, shared, "This eviction may be the best thing that could possibly happen to them… it's the wake-up call they need!"

My friend, Nick Spohn, noted:

> To be godly is to be in a position of service. Being a landlord is no exception. We must happily serve our customers (tenants) and do what we can to maintain a good relationship. After all, we are leaving our assets in their hands. It's not our job to give a handout or enable bad behavior. Land-lording is a tough business, and setting crystal clear expectations ahead of time—in a contract—and then holding them to it is the only possible way to prosper. Unfortunately, that often means evicting someone who is either not paying or not taking care of our property. While our hearts want to help them and give them leeway, our checkbooks and emotional health will get punished if we do that. Holding people to their word is vital to being a successful investor, and if you can't hold

strong boundaries, this may not be the business for you. We can serve more people by making sound financial and business decisions. That often means drawing a hard line with what type of behaviors we will tolerate. Tough love is still love. Every bad tenant you think you're helping is a great tenant you're not serving.

Yes! The longer we carry a person's load, the less effective we become in carrying our own.

My good friend, Joe Cantu, aims to help people in any way he can, including a bad tenant. He shared, "Just because the transaction failed doesn't mean we should be treating the person any differently. However, we must be good stewards of the assets that God gave us. If we let the tenant live there for free, we're not doing them any favors. We're only enabling them." We must ask ourselves not just "What would Jesus do?" but instead ask "What would we do if this person was Jesus? Could we be respectful, helpful, and kind... even as we were escorting them out?" I believe we can.

My final interview was with a local friend, Ted. He described how he sets clear boundaries both in his lease agreements as well as in his business ethics. In one way, God uses Ted to help a tenant get through a rough stage in their life. In another way, He uses Ted to help another tenant by evicting them, so the tenant learns to be accountable. He says it's on a case-by-case basis. And he always asks God what is the best move: *God, are you using me to help this person to get through a financial hardship, or do I need to help them by holding them to the agreement?*

When asked how he would handle a nonperforming tenant, Ted says, "I give them one month reprieve. If they don't pay, I must move forward with the eviction. Or, I can add $100 a month to their monthly payment until they're caught up or spread it out over two months. But if they break that agreement, I can't help them anymore. They haven't held up their end of the bargain. So, they have to go!"

In each interaction, Ted asks himself: *Am I showing this tenant love and grace? Or am I the one in the crowd shouting, "Crucify Him, crucify Him, crucify Him"?*

When tension rises and things aren't going as planned, Ted calls to the father and says, "I don't like this feeling of anger." And the Holy Spirit answers, "Do you believe that I am God and that I'll take care of you? How do you know I'm not using you to help this family? Is it their money that you need? Or do you need to do the will of God?" Powerful! Ted aims to impact a tenant's experience so greatly that his tenant may reflect back and think, *Wow! There really is a God!* God is using Ted to impact the lives of others.

What impact will you have on your tenants?

SUMMARY JUDGMENT

We opened this chapter with two parables: one of grace and one of truth. We need to forgive. We also need to set property boundaries. Each situation is unique, just like the stories in the two parables. We must ask God if our unique situation calls for grace, truth, or a mix of both. How do we balance the bar of truth and grace? That will be for the judge to decide.

CHAPTER 7

The People versus Property: An Eviction Case

Don't let negative people live in your head. Raise the rent and kick them out.[1]

—ROBERT TEW

In the last chapter, we described how there is a time to forgive and a time to enforce a boundary. Knowing when to offer grace and when to speak the truth can be a balancing act in and of itself. Now that you understand the principles, I'd like to share some personal examples of balancing grace and truth to enforce a boundary line.

THE PROPERTY WITHOUT A PRAYER: TOO MUCH TRUTH

Evictions often turn into screaming matches. That was the case for me after I placed a seventy-two-hour notice to vacate letter on the door of my first property back in chapter two. The tenant called me screaming, "I'm not leaving. You'll have to evict me." But just because someone is yelling and screaming at us doesn't necessarily mean something is wrong. It's actually a good thing because they are learning they cannot act this way and get away with it. They can yell and scream all they'd like. It doesn't mean we have to respond in kind.

As nerve-racking as it sounds to take someone to court, it's actually a very streamlined process—even in some of the more tenant-friendly states. It may just take longer and require you to jump through a few more hoops if you reside in one of these tenant-friendly states. But you have nothing to worry about in the case of nonpayment—you will always win! My first eviction at my first property was in Texas—a very landlord-friendly state. It took about three weeks to get a court date scheduled. The judge ruled in our favor and gave the tenant five days to move out.

"What about the money they owe me?" I asked the county clerk while exiting the courtroom.

"Well, you can always file a judgment lien against them for the amount they owe you. Every time the tenant goes to apply for a new loan, the creditor will see the tenant owes you money," the clerk suggested.

"Let's do it! That'll show 'em," I responded with pride.

This was obviously more truth than grace. I wasn't strong in my faith at the time. Forgiveness was not in my vocabulary.

As I reflect on this, I must ask, *Was that really the right move?* After all, I had already gotten what I wanted—they were out! Did it hurt to lose one month's rent? Sure. But it certainly didn't harm me in the long run. Filing this judgment lien didn't do me any good anyway: I never recovered the money. I only did it out of spite.

Offering so much truth with no grace backfired. Not only did it harm the tenant from getting future credit, I now have a lien attached to my property that I must clear before I can sell it, ultimately creating more paperwork and legal fees to remove it.

So… who won?

THE PROPERTY WITHOUT A PRAYER: TOO MUCH GRACE

One month after signing a lease with my qualified tenant at my first property, I received am email from a local landlord asking for an honest review of my quirky tenant—the one who busted the hose spigot and flooded the front yard on the last day of her lease. My gut reaction was to ignore the request. It's better to say nothing than to share how I really felt. I was protecting my ego from being hurt: Why should I help her?

But God reminded me I serve Him by serving others. After all, what's the harm in sharing highlights of truth: the quirky tenant *did* pay on time, she *did* stay for three years, and she never had any complaints from the police or neighbors. At this point, she was out of my life. Sure, she caused stress and anxiety in the final days. But protecting my ego from hurt would only cause her harm in the end. I informed the fellow landlord that she stayed for three years and always paid on time, but we just chose not to renew her lease. This was no doubt too much grace and no truth. Equally poisonous!

FASTER THAN A NEW YORK NO!

I recently closed a deal in New York using a sandwich lease option (see chapter nine). The seller had a tenant who'd stopped paying rent three months prior. I agreed to assist in the eviction before closing. I'm okay with being the bad guy. We gave her thirty days' notice, then fourteen days, then three. On the last day, she was still in the house. No surprise.

"My boyfriend is really screwing me. Can I stay here for just another month until I move out of state?"

Without a second thought, I leveraged the most powerful one-word boundary: "No!"

If I contemplated it any further, I would not be honoring my own personal boundary, nor would I be honoring my family's financial well-being. I'd be losing; she'd be winning. I can't eat *for* her. And, as heartless as that may appear, I did not put her in that position. I didn't need to carry her load. I can't grow for her; only she can. I'm grateful to have set the right boundary at the right time. During the formal eviction process, I learned the seller's tenant had been evicted from the past three properties. One property she burned to the ground!

THE TENNESSEE TWO-FER

I have a property in Tennessee that sat vacant for months. I accepted a quack out of desperation. Within two months, it became clear she couldn't afford the monthly payment. I only accepted her because she had a roommate with a second source of income. I gave the tenant thirty days to find another place and offered her cash for keys. "If you can prove you're 100 percent moved out in the next thirty days, I will give you $1,000." Well, one month passed, and she hadn't left.

So, I placed the property back on the market to find another tenant. One of the first prospect calls I received was from a broker who was helping one of his older clients find a home. I explained that it could be another forty-five days before we could show the property because I was in the middle of eviction. He proposed a rather intriguing solution:

"Give me your tenant's phone number. I'll call and ask if she's open to having my client as a roommate. It's an all-around win: You don't have to evict, my client gets in, your tenant gets to stay, and they can share the monthly expenses."

"I love that idea. Very creative. Let me first contact my tenant and see if she'd be open to that," I said.

Immediately after our call, I began thinking: *Wait a minute. My tenant hasn't been able to make a full month's payment in two months. Why do I need to come in and save her? If I let her stay, I'm only enabling her.* I was trying to eat for her. If I allowed this to continue, she would be irresponsible and happy, and I would be responsible and miserable.[2] Again,

I had to practice the strongest one-word boundary in the dictionary: *No!*

"Responsibility is a gift of enormous value."[3]

CASE DISMISSED

People matter, especially those who aren't able to carry their own load. There's a reason why they're not performing. And the reason is much bigger than you. They have a lot of things going on that are out of their control. They're not trying to spite you or intentionally trying to take advantage of you. We can be a steward to those in troubled times by either offering grace or truth. How much of each depends on the circumstance.

Remember, just because the transaction failed doesn't mean they're a bad person. They still deserve respect and empathy. We must give our tenants as much grace as we do truth. Everyone experiences hardships. How can you help them get back on their feet? How could you ensure they're set up to succeed in their next residence? What does grace (undeserved love) look like in this situation?

Here are just a few ways to ethically serve people even as you're serving an eviction notice:

- Communicate in advance your intentions to evict. This shouldn't come as a surprise to them.
- Offer cash in exchange for keys in lieu of having an eviction appear on their record.
- Offer to pay for their moving truck.

- Give them some or all their deposit back. They need the money more than you do.
- Give them a letter of recommendation highlighting their positive attributes.

There's a fine line between helping them manage and being taken advantage. An eviction isn't bad. It's a new beginning; a fresh start for the tenant and a new opportunity for you as the investor to provide a new home to a new family.

I run a business to support my family and serve people in need. But, when the first is sacrificed for the second, then my ability to serve others is diminished. Yet, with the right boundaries in place, you're able to serve based on each of your tenant's specific circumstances. You can waive late fees or work out a payment plan, all out of the kindness of your heart versus out of obligation. In 2 Corinthians 9:7, it reminds us that God loves a cheerful giver. We are in control of our giving. "Favors and sacrifices are a part of the Christian life. Enabling is not."[4]

Case dismissed.

SECTION THREE:

PROPERTY

The Good Steward of Property

If you buy one property this year, two properties next year, three the following year, four in year four, and five properties in the fifth year—you'll have fifteen rental properties at an average of $400 a month cash flow: $6,000 a month! How would that change your life?[1]

—DUSTIN HEINER

TIME, TALENTS, AND TREASURE

In Matthew 25: 14–30, Jesus tells a story of a man taking a long trip. Before his departure, he gave three of his servants three different amounts of money based on their abilities. Upon his return, the man called on his servants to account for his money. Two of the servants managed to double and triple the amount they'd been given, to which the man replied, "You have been faithful over this small amount, so now I will give you much more."[2]

But the third servant feared the man and didn't want to put the money at risk, so the servant buried the money. The man was furious! "You should at least have put my money into the bank so I could have some interest."[3] For the man who uses well what he is given shall be given more, and he shall have abundance.[4]

When I first began investing, I used traditional financing and put 20 percent down to buy the property. The down payment remained trapped until I either sold the property or refinanced it. In the next phase of my investing career, I was buying with 100 percent cash. I was like the third servant in Jesus's parable: playing it safe.

I wanted to be a good steward of the money my master gave me. I believe any wise investment in real estate is far better than burying your money in the ground. However, I was using only the talents I learned as a beginner investor. I hadn't yet developed the talent of using other people's property and other people's debt.

In this chapter, I will share my personal experience with four investing strategies: buy and hold, BRRRR, (buy, rehab, refinance, rent, and repeat), fix and flip, and the cash purchase. I'm not advocating any one strategy over the other. These methods are how I entered the realm of real estate. Your strategy will be unique based on your level of capital, your risk tolerance, your time availability, the talent you already possess, and the talent you seek to develop.

As you read these next two chapters, you must ask yourself (or your master): *What is the best use of my time, talent, and treasure?*

THE GOOD STEWARD OF PROPERTY: BURYING MONEY

BURYING MONEY: BUY AND HOLD

I had full intentions to produce enough passive income to quit my day job *someday*. I saw the possibility of *how*. I just didn't know *when*. My wife just had a baby, and we were living paycheck to paycheck. Lynn desperately wanted to stay home and raise our newborn baby herself versus paying $1,200 a month in childcare. Our combined retirement accounts only added up to about $150,000. Not bad. But it certainly wasn't enough to retire at the age of thirty-seven!

My mentor at the time, David Fisher, told me, "If you want to get to Disneyland, follow someone who's been." He showed me a loophole in the US tax law that allows you to access your retirement savings penalty-free before the age of fifty-nine and a half. It's known as a Qualified Domestic Relations Order (QDRO). Essentially, it's a separation of assets between a married couple. These are common in divorce decrees when one spouse is owed a portion of the other's retirement assets.

The divorce attorney presents the QDRO to a county judge for approval, which is then sent to the employer's retirement plan administrator for distribution. The plan administrator creates a separate retirement account for the receiving spouse. The receiving spouse has the choice to invest it however they wish or distribute some or all the proceeds—penalty-free!

"Lynn, we're getting a divorce!" I announced to my wife.

As you can imagine, that did not sit well with her. So, I had my real estate attorney explain it to her instead.

"There's no divorce decree needed. All we're doing is requesting a separation of assets," he assured her.

Since the retirement funds have never been taxed, the plan administrator withholds 20 percent to send to the IRS since retirement accounts are tax-deferred funds. However, by investing in real estate, the investment appears as a loss on paper when you file your taxes. Therefore, you will get most, if not all, of the amount the IRS withheld back as a tax return when you file taxes for that calendar year (depending on your current tax situation, of course).

Not bad when you consider the alternative of borrowing against your retirement plan only to have to pay it back with interest! Within eighteen months, we purchased five properties with an average cash flow of $400 per month. The cash flow we received didn't replace Lynn's income, but it was just enough to keep us above water.

$150,000 in retirement accounts ÷ $30,000 average
cost per property = five rental properties

$400 a month free cash flow per property × five
rental properties = $2,000 a month cash flow

Though I wasn't walking with God at the time, I know He was watching out for my family's well-being. Within two years of my investment career, Lynn quit her job. Mission accomplished! But what about me? I want to quit too! My plan was to work in corporate America for another ten years and build up my retirement savings again to purchase five more properties. But ten years? Ugh! Something didn't seem right. Stay tuned, because in chapter nine, I will show you how to become an even better steward of property.

Table 8.1 below displays the good, the bad, and the ugly of using the buy and hold method.

BUY & HOLD WITH TRADITIONAL FINANCING		
The Good	**The Bad**	**The Ugly**
Typically turn-key (move in ready); no rehab required	Large down payment required for non-owner-occupied properties	Lenders may not be willing to extend loans if you do not have W2 income; maximum amount of 10 traditional loans
Re-fi 'til you die! As the market price and rental rates increase, you can refinance and still received a monthly cashflow spread	Lenders require a certain credit score to qualify for financing	Your large down payment stays trapped within the property until you sell or refinance

But what if you don't have a retirement account? What if you're not married and, therefore, cannot leverage the QRDO to tap into your retirement account penalty-free? The fix and flip and BRRRR model discussed below allow you to purchase a property, fix it, and either sell it or rent it.

Yet, both strategies still require money.

The fix and flip and BRRRR methods are similar in nature except for one major difference: your exit strategy. With fix and flip, your exit strategy is to sell the property. With BRRRR, your exit is to rent it; you stay in the deal.

I purchased my first three rental properties using traditional bank financing. These were turn-key, rent-ready properties, no rehab required. On my fourth property, I learned about hard money the easy way. On my fifth property, I learned about hard money the hard way.

A hard money loan is a short-term private money loan that allows you to purchase and renovate fixer-upper properties. The loan typically comes at a much higher interest rate than that of a traditional loan. Don't be fooled by the term "hard money." It's easy to get but can sometimes be hard to get out if you can't sell the property.

Will your rehab costs increase? Will you stay within the budget? Will your complete your rehab in the allotted time? Will the property appraise at the estimated value? Will you be able to sell it quickly enough at the appraised price without discounting it? Will a global pandemic shut down materials production? There are so many factors outside of your control.

My first mentoring group included access to investor-friendly realtors. One realtor presented my fourth rental property as an easy rehab. In its as-is condition, it wasn't shiny and glossy like some of the other already-flipped houses in the area.

Nonetheless, it was livable and no doubt *rentable*. I was up for the challenge of flipping a house.

It cost me $15,000 cash out of pocket to close the hard money side of the transaction and another $6,000 to refinance to a conventional loan. Total cash out of pocket: $21,000. The hard money lender loaned me the funds to replace the roof, paint the interior and exterior, replace the HVAC unit, and replace the flooring. My mentoring group connected me with the right contractors. In less than seven days, the rehab was complete.

"I'm a house flipper!" I proudly exclaimed to my wife.

Once rehabbed, I could have sold it and gotten all my money back. Maybe I should have. Or, I could have just rented it as-is without the headache of a rehab project. By rehabilitating it, however, the value of the property increased from $120,000 to $160,000 with just $20,000 in updates. Wow! A $40,000 in equity capture. That's amazing!

Is it though? What is *equity capture* anyway? It's a beautiful thing if I intended to sell the property right away and capture that equity in the form of profit. But my intent with this property was to hold it and rent it out; therefore, the equity I "captured" remained unrealized until I sell.

Here's why I believe it was a crummy tradeoff: after completing the rehab, I refinanced out of the 14 percent hard money loan to a traditional loan at a 5 percent interest rate. The new lender extended a loan for $128,000 (i.e., 80 percent of the $160,000 appraised value). Now I was responsible for making a monthly payment to a loan of $128,000. I could have just applied for a traditional loan at the original $100,000 purchase price and had a lower monthly payment!

The property would have qualified for traditional loan. There was no major rehab required. My rehab simply made the house sparkle and shine. The benefit of performing the renovations initially was that the hard money lender foot the bill for the rehab costs. So not a total loss. Within forty-five days, we had it rented at the highest market price in the neighborhood. *Yes!*

Still riding the high of my first BRRR project, I was ready to repeat the process. Property number five is where I learned the greatest lesson: I'm not a flipper—nor did I want to be! This property required an extensive amount of work. It would not qualify for a traditional loan in its current condition. I cut corners and did most of the work myself. The time away from my family added so much stress that it almost ended my marriage!

The hard money closing cost was $23,000. After exceeding my budget and going over the allotted time schedule, the property appraised $15,000 *less than* what I'd estimated, which added another $15,000 to the conventional loan refinance expense. *Grrrr!* What should have been a $23,000 total cash out of pocket ended up being $37,000. Never again!

Table 8.2 is a snapshot summarizing the good, the bad, and the ugly side of the BRRRR and the fix and flip model.

B.R.R.R.R. AND FIX & FLIP		
The Good	**The Bad**	**The Ugly**
No credit score required to obtain a hard-money loan	Good credit score required if you plan to refinance and rent	Rehab cost increase; property appraisal comes in lower than anticipated
Other investors, known as wholesalers, bring deals to you	Wholesalers profit may hinder the deal from being profitable	Unable to find a buyer at your preferred price; hard money lender forecloses on you if you can't sell
Large profit "potential"	Often limited to larger metro areas where investor/cash buyers are active	Paying high interest rates to borrow money; paying "carrying costs" during rehab (utilities, insurance, taxes, interest)

Even with the dismal outcome of the second flip that flopped, the real estate bug had bitten me. It was an itch I couldn't help but scratch. Yet, at this point, I was all out of money and all out of energy. I was done investing for a while. Or, so I thought.

BURYING MONEY: CASH PURCHASE

Mortgage lenders allow you up to ten traditional mortgages at one time before cutting you off. So, scaling your business by using traditional financing is out of the question. You could buy all your properties with cash. But, regardless of how much money you have, you'll eventually run out if you bury all your money in investment properties.

Nonetheless, if you have the money to spare and you do not wish to hassle with mortgage lenders, purchasing with all cash is a viable option. I used bank financing to acquire my first five properties. My next five investments were purchased with cash saved up in my emergency fund. In retrospect, I can't say that buying more investment properties qualified as an *emergency.*

On the plus side, paying cash and, thus, not having a mortgage means you get to keep more of the monthly payment from your tenants. I say "monthly payment" versus cash flow intentionally because cash flow is profit. Your monthly payment isn't profit *yet.* It's a payback of principal that you already put out when you purchased with all cash.

As I developed more talents by learning more creative ways to purchase, I realized there were better ways to invest versus burying all my money in real estate deals. Nowadays, buying all cash no longer makes sense to me.

- It's too expensive!
- It's too much money tied up in the property.
- It takes too long to get paid back.

Nonetheless, buying with cash certainly gives you more options for your exit strategy. Once you've purchased the property with all cash, you can:

- Sell it *as-is* for a higher price with a realtor
    - You may be better off wholesaling it and saving yourself the initial cash outlay (see chapter nine).

- Rehab and sell it at a higher price
    - You might as well pursue a hard money lender to fund the rehab costs (discussed above).
- Rehab and offer it as a short-term Airbnb or as a long-term rental
    - You might consider using the BRRRR strategy to leverage other people's money for the rehab costs (discussed above).
- Delayed financing
    - Purchase with cash to negotiate the lowest purchase price with the seller, make minimal repairs (if any) to ensure it would pass a mortgage lender's inspection, apply for a new mortgage loan to get *most* of your cash back, then begin paying the new conventional lender a monthly mortgage payment, and repeat.
- Offer it as a rent-to-own home to a tenant-buyer in its as-is condition
    - My favorite

A cash purchase gives you more control. Yet, it creates a high opportunity cost by burying your money, diminishing its use for other investment opportunities. A cash purchase is better than "digging a hole in the ground and hiding it for safekeeping." If nothing else, you're heeding the master's advice and gaining some interest by investing in real estate.

Table 8.3 summarizes the pros and cons of a cash purchase.

CASH PURCHASE		
The Good	**The Bad**	**The Ugly**
Money talks: negotiate a very low price	Opportunity cost: all the equity is tied up in the property	Property's condition could be far beyond repair
No bank qualifying	Payback period is longer	The property may not sell and all your cash is tied up in to the property
Lower closing cost: no bank loan originating fees	Investor-cash buyers typically pay all closing costs that are normally paid for by the seller	Seller's loan balance may prevent a low purchase price

THE GOOD STEWARD DID WHAT HE THOUGHT BEST BASED ON HIS ABILITY

After reading these stories, you might think I am against the strategies described in this chapter. Not at all! Many investors I know still leverage these methods today and do quite well. You also might assume that these paths are how you must enter into real estate. Absolutely not. I share these strategies in the order in which I enter the real estate world. Your path may be completely different, especially after reading the next chapter.

What if you don't have a treasure chest of money lying around like the man in Jesus's parable? You may just be starting out. You may be like me and don't want to wait another ten years before you can quit your job. Luckily, there are more talents you can gain if you're willing to put in the time.

In the next chapter, you'll learn more fruitful avenues in which you can double or triple your master's earnings in very little time by becoming a better steward of property. As you master more methods, you suddenly realize there's no need to bury all your money in real estate.

STRATEGIES SUMMARY

The purpose of this chapter was to provide you with investment strategies if you're seeking to take a more active approach to real estate investing. Personally, I vote you stick to passive strategies where you do all the work upfront and get paid in monthly increments, so you don't have to worry about when your next payday will arrive. It takes just as much work (if not more) to complete any of these nonpassive strategies and get paid once than it does to complete a creative finance deal and receive paydays every month for years to come! Time becomes your biggest asset, and you learn to treasure each moment.

Table 8.4 captures the benefits and downfalls of each of the strategies we discussed in this chapter.

	The Good	The Bad	The Ugly
B.R.R.R.R.	No credit score required to obtain a hard-money loan	Limited to larger metro areas where investor/cash buyers are active	Rehab cost increase; property appraisal comes in lower than anticipated
Fix & Flip	Quick turn around to capture profit (3-6 months)	Profit is taxed at the highest tax bracket	Property doesn't sell; you're stuck in a high interest hard money loan

CHAPTER 9

The Better Steward of Property

Real estate is for producing cash, not burying it.[1]

—BLAIR HALVER

THE BRAVE STEWARD

Before leaving the country, the man in Jesus's parable gave his second servant more money than he did the third servant as he felt the second servant possessed greater ability. Upon his return, the man was pleased to find the second servant managed to double his master's money. To which the man replied, "You have been faithful over this small amount, so now I will give you much more."[2]

In the last chapter, you learned some of the traditional methods of real estate investing, which required a significant outlay of cash. But what if you don't have money in the bank to put a 20 percent down payment on a house, let alone 100 percent down payment with a cash purchase? What if you don't have a good credit score to even qualify for a bank loan? What if you don't want to become entangled in a hefty rehab project?

Answer: You must become a better steward of your master's money.

When I first started investing, I didn't know about wholesaling or novations, which allow you to earn a profit without ever owning real estate. Essentially, you sign a contract with a seller, you assign that contract to another party, they execute that contract, and you earn an assignment fee.

THE BRAVE STEWARD: WHOLESALING

If you have the time to learn the skill of wholesaling, you can make money. But it takes time.

Wholesaling has a low financial barrier to entry. Your only upfront costs are the marketing dollars. The profits could be large. However, the average wholesale profit ranges between $5,000 to $10,000, which is why it's not my favorite play. An investor once told me, "You're spending the same amount of time each day either way. Why not get paid *more* for that time?"

After experiencing my first successful flip and flop with my fourth and fifth properties, not to mention burying all my cash in five more properties, I thought, *There has to be another way!* On properties four and five, I noticed there was no realtor representing the seller. Instead, my realtor was coordinating with a *wholesaler*, who apparently finds properties at a deep discount. The wholesaler signs a contract directly with the seller and then sells the rights to execute that contract to another investor for a fee.

I was intrigued and wanted to understand how this wholesaler middleman was able to find a deal, connect with another investor or realtor, and make a profit. The wholesaler is connecting buyers and sellers for a fee—like that of a realtor but *without* having to hold a real estate license! How were they doing it? How did they get into it? How do they find deals?

In the words of my first mentor, David Fisher, "If you want to get to Disneyland, follow someone who's been." I contacted each of these wholesalers from my prior two properties to learn more. Within a few months, I was on the hunt for my first wholesale deal.

In chapter ten, we'll dive deeper into the details, and even the disasters, of each deal structure covered in this chapter. In the meantime, you can use table 9.1 to evaluate the bonuses as well as the burdens that are born with wholesaling.

WHOLESALE		
The Good	**The Bad**	**The Ugly**
Low-cost barrier to entry to get started	Time-intensive (active vs. passive Income)	Required to make low-ball offers; profiting from others' hardships and/or lack of knowledge
Minimal risk; profit without owning	Non-steady Income	Hindered in some states
Seller and buyer do not see your profit	Limited to larger metro areas where investor/cash buyers are active	Unable to find an end buyer (investor, cash buyer, or owner/occupant)

A novation is similar to wholesaling, but instead of assigning away your rights to execute the purchase contract, you replace your name with the end buyer's name. However, unlike wholesaling, the seller grants you permission to list the property on the market as well as sign the contract documents for them. You become the seller's attorney-in-fact (AIF), which grants you the legal right to either list the property yourself using a flat-fee real estate broker or hire a real estate agent to list the property for you.

Pro tip: Hire a real estate agent. They are experienced in fielding buyers' agents. They know the lingo. They know the laws. I listed a property myself using a flat-fee broker service and was inundated with buyer agents' calls, questions, and hassles. Never again!

Just like wholesaling, in a novation, you—as the middleman—agree to pay the seller's closing cost and all agents' fees. The price you and the seller agree upon is the price he or she will receive at the closing table. No surprises.

Novations differ from wholesaling in that the end buyer is typically an owner-occupant—not an investor. Since you will be listing the property on the local multiple listing service (MLS), you can expect to attract a buyer who desires to live in the property.

MAKING CENTS OF A NOVATION

A novation will make sense if the seller truly wants to be hands-off. They don't want to deal with real estate agents. They don't want to talk to buyers. They may have already moved out of state. Essentially, they are emotionally disconnected from the property and ready to let it go. At the same time, they aren't willing to let their property go at a deeply discounted *wholesale* price. They know what their property is worth, and they know they can get a higher price. If the property is in a rural area where there is not a large amount of investor/cash buyer activity, a novation could make sense.

A novation will not make sense if the seller wants to play an active role. They also understand they could hire a real estate agent themselves. Many sellers have even asked me, "Why do I need you? I could just list it myself." Ninety-nine!

You approach novations in two ways depending on the condition of the property:

- Move-in ready
- Rehab required

MOVE-IN READY

If the property does not have major safety issues and would pass a mortgage lender's inspection in its current condition, you can hire a real estate agent to list it as-is. Some minor work may be needed—just nothing that would scare off your average qualified buyer.

REHAB REQUIRED

Contrary to the fix and flip or BRRRR method discussed in chapter eight, a novation structure allows you to perform any rehab needed to attract the highest sale price possible *while the seller still owns the property*! This means you don't need to apply for a hard money loan and pay insanely high interest rates.

However, it does mean you foot the bill for rehab expenses. Why would you do that? Typically, the profit you expect to earn from the final sale will cover whatever expenses you incur. *But what if the seller reneges on the agreement halfway through?* This is a valid concern. You set the expectation with the seller that you're going to begin investing money into this, and if they back out, they will be responsible for reimbursement.

If the seller backs out, you have the legal right to seek remuneration. You place a lien on the property so that if and when the seller sells to another party, your company's name appears on the title as a lienholder that must be paid off before a clear title can transfer to a new owner.

I've never had to do this because I only work with sellers I deem as valuable business partners. I don't jump into business partnerships with people who do not want to do business with me, which typically becomes apparent within the first few interactions.

I'll share a few case studies in the next chapter in hopes of bringing more clarity to this concept of novation. For now, you can review table 9.2, which summarizes the value and the variables of a novation arrangement.

"NOVATION" VS. "WHOLESALE"		
The Good	**The Bad**	**The Ugly**
Offer a higher price to sellers vs. traditional wholesaling	Time intensive (active vs. passive income)	Deal falls through halfway after you've invested money in the rehab
Profit without owning; higher profit potential vs. wholesaling	Requires seller to give you power of attorney or attorney In fact	You must cloud the title and seek legal remuneration if the deal fails
Less risk and less cash outlay than fix & flip	Non-steady income (active vs. passive income)	Most title companies aren't aware of this method
Not limited to larger metro areas; works in smaller cities because you sell to owner/occupants	The seller's mindset is: "I can list it myself. Why do I need you?"	End buyers are pickier and more meticulous than investor/cash buyers that typically work with wholesalers
You hire a seller's agent to do all the leg work for you	You pay closing costs & realtor fees	You may not find an end buyer willing to pay your asking price
Full transparency: seller, buyer, and realtor see everything (no sneakiness)	Full transparency: seller, buyer, and realtor see everything (your profit is exposed)	Full transparency: seller, buyer, and realtor see everything (and expect larger concessions)

Just as I realized how I was burying all my master's money in real estate with buy and hold, fix and flip, and cash purchases, I also realized how I was burying all my *time* in searching for new wholesale and novation deals. I'd get a deal, sell it, get paid, then have to start all over again. I was trading time for money, exactly like I'd been doing in corporate America! It felt like the rat race of real estate investing.

I didn't yet understand the power and scalability of creative financing.

THE BOLD STEWARD

As cash on hand dwindled, I had to become a better steward of the assets.

Over a period of six years, I purchased twenty-five properties. In year one and two, I bought my first five rentals using $150,000 of retirement savings using the buy and hold and BRRRR method. In year three, I purchased five more properties using $75,000 cash. In year four, I acquired five more but only used $35,000 with a little more creativity. In year five, I obtained five more properties with $17,000. Now, in year six of my investing career, I am picking up five additional properties but with only $8,000 total cash out of pocket.

I strongly desired to be like the first steward in Jesus's parable who did not fear his master; whose master trusted him with great assets; who managed to triple his master's earnings and was granted even more! That's when I discovered an even better way to purchase property without applying for loans, without burying all my money (and time) in deals, and without worrying about when my next payday was coming.

That's when I was introduced to creative financing: owner financing, subject to, and the sandwich lease purchase. Let's explore each briefly.

THE BOLD STEWARD: OWNER FINANCE

This is by far the safest creative financing strategy because there is no underlying mortgage on the property. The seller owns the property free and clear. When you purchase, the title transfers out of the seller's name, and the seller becomes the bank. The attorney or title company creates a mortgage note showing the schedule of payments to be made, which the seller may use as collateral to foreclose and take the property back in case of default.

Most sellers who are familiar with owner financing will demand a high-interest rate. And rightfully so, since they are taking a risk of you possibly defaulting. If you agree to pay the seller interest, you must send them a tax form each year or pay an escrow company to keep tabs on principal and interest payments. Better yet, you can avoid that hassle and negotiate a 0 percent interest rate and instead agree upon a monthly payment that both you and the seller can accept.

Table 9.3 is a quick summary of the pros and cons of owner financing.

OWNER FINANCE		
The Good	**The Bad**	**The Ugly**
Minimal money down; more profit potential	Only works if the seller doesn't need all their money right now to purchase another property	Inherit deferred maintenance if the seller hasn't kept up on the property
No bank qualifying; quicker closing	Seller may demand a higher interest rate for carrying the mortgage note	The condition of the property may hinder your ability to qualify for a new loan; regardless of how many repairs are performed

THE BOLD STEWARD: SUBJECT TO

Subject to (also known as sub2) is, by far, my favorite strategy. This method was first introduced to me by Ron LeGrand, then later by Blair Halver, Robert Paschal, and Pace Morby.

Subject to *what*, you might ask?

You purchase the property, and the title transfers to you *subject to* the seller's mortgage loan staying in the sellers name for a few years (or indefinitely).

Why would a seller do that?

Most sellers I help have experienced some sort of hardship and just want out. They have a mortgage payment they either have stopped paying or can no longer afford to pay. Or they don't want to list the property with a real estate agent, which could take several months. Perhaps the seller may not have enough equity in the property to pay the agent's commissions and closing costs. They may not have kept up with the maintenance and repairs for some time. The real estate agent might have told them they needed to make repairs first before listing it.

These sellers who are open to a sub2 purchase do not have the money, the time, or the mental bandwidth to sell their property using traditional methods. That's where you and I show up with a creative solution.

You purchase the property as-is, deferred maintenance and all. You agree to catch up on their mortgage loan payments if they are behind. Thus, the seller avoids a bank foreclosure, which—by the way—is the worst thing they could experience if they ever hope to obtain a future line of credit.

The title of the property transfers out of the seller's name, and the seller moves out of the property. You now own the property. Yet, the loan stays in the seller's name. You agree to make the seller's loan payments to their mortgage company until paid—or until an agreed-upon time in the future. You can sweeten the deal by giving them a small down payment to help with the cost of moving expenses.

I'll share more in the next chapter about the mechanics of sub2. In the meantime, you can use table 9.4 below as a snapshot of weighing the ups and downs of sub2 deals.

SUBJECT-TO		
The Good	**The Bad**	**The Ugly**
Minimal money down; More profit potential	Lender may call loan due if they discover a sale has occurred	Inherit deferred maintenance
No bank qualifying	Seller's credit is impacted if you default	Seller may file bankruptcy; home could be seized, and you're forced to refinance
Quicker closing; no bank loan approvals	Only works if the seller doesn't need all their money upfront to purchase another property	Seller passes away and you're forced to refinance or enter into litigation with the heirs
Seller may have a more favorable interest rate than the prevailing interest rate	Seller may have a less favorable interest rate than the prevailing interest rate	The condition of the property may hinder your ability to qualify for a new loan; regardless of how many repairs are performed

THE BOLD STEWARD: SANDWICH LEASE PURCHASE

Let's say the seller is not in financial distress, and they don't trust you to make their mortgage payment. Their situation may not match many of the seller's circumstances described in table 3.1 of chapter three. At the same time, they need to sell and may have exhausted their other options. If that is the case, you can ask them if they'd be willing to rent the property to you and give you the option to purchase it down the road. Enter the sandwich lease purchase. The best way to describe a sandwich lease purchase is a lease within a lease. There are three players in this scenario:

Party A—Seller
Party B—Investor (you)
Party C—Tenant-buyer

You (party B) lease the property from the seller (party A). And within that lease, you include a clause that allows you to sub-lease the property to your tenant-buyer (party C). You are sandwiched in the middle (A-B-C). You have the *option* to purchase the property at the end of the lease period for a predetermined price that you and the seller have agreed upon in advance.

Notice the word *option*.

You have the option to purchase the property. That doesn't mean you have an *obligation* to purchase. The seller can't force you to buy. But, if at the end of the term, you do not buy, the seller has the right to regain control of the property.

Obviously, you would never want to enter a sandwich lease purchase with the intention of *not* fulfilling your commitment. As the buyer, you have the *right* to exercise your option to purchase (not the *obligation*). Contrastingly, the seller does have the *obligation* to sell you the property based on the terms of the contract. Nevertheless, please understand that *everything* in real estate is negotiable.

You give your tenant-buyer (party C) an *option* to purchase the property from you (party B), and you have an *obligation* to sell to the tenant-buyer. You structure the option period with the seller (A–B) to be five years and the option period between you and your tenant-buyer (B–C) to be one to two years. This buffer of time acts as a safety net in case your tenant-buyer needs more time to execute their purchase or you have to find another tenant-buyer.

If your tenant-buyer is unable to exercise their option to purchase at the end of the one- or two-year term, their option to purchase expires. Typically, they (or the property) are not "loan-ready." They may not have completed the credit repair program, or they did not fix the property as promised. So, a mortgage lender will not extend a loan either because their credit score is too low or the condition of the property doesn't meet a lender's requirements.

Ultimately, the tenant-buyer lost their right to purchase. But that doesn't necessarily mean they need to leave. You can create a new lease with new terms: a new monthly payment, a new purchase price, and a new option period.

If, at the end of the new term, the tenant-buyer is still not ready, you can renegotiate the terms of the contract with the seller. The seller doesn't have to accept these terms and can certainly take possession of the property once again. But the aim is to never get to the point where the seller is so upset they demand control of their house back. That's why you first learned in chapter four to only conduct business with sellers who are partners.

You treat your sellers and tenant-buyers as partners instead of pawn pieces in your game of real estate chess. Communication is key. Therefore, you'll be in constant communication with both partners. Successful partners communicate, check in with one another along the way, and ensure the end goal of *purchasing* is achieved.

Table 9.5 displays the good, the bad, and the ugly side of the sandwich lease-purchase arrangement.

SANDWICH LEASE PURCHASE		
The Good	**The Bad**	**The Ugly**
Seller is responsible for major repairs because they still own the property and hold legal title	Since seller still owns the property, you don't get to claim any tax benefits (depreciation deduction)	Since seller still owns the property, they can default on their monthly mortgage payment or place a lien on the property. You may not find out until it's too late
No bank qualifying; quicker closing	Seller still controls the property; they can more easily renege on the deal	Seller backs out and chooses not to sell; litigation ensues between you and the seller and/or you and your tenant-buyer

In the next chapter, we'll discuss more of the do's and don'ts of this sandwich lease purchase method.

THE BETTER STEWARD OF PROPERTY

No single investment strategy is right for everyone. The best strategy is the one you're most likely to implement based on your risk tolerance, your timeframe, the money you have to invest, and your exit strategy.

As my talents (i.e., skill level) grew, I became an even better steward of talents (i.e., assets). No longer did I behave like the third steward who buried his master's money in the ground with large down payments or cash purchases. I was able to leverage other people's property via the sandwich lease purchase and even utilize other people's debt via sub2 to cast a wider net and help more people in need while at the same time doubling or tripling my master's money to have a greater impact.

Jesus wrapped up the parable of the talents by saying, "For the man who uses well what he is given shall be given more, and he shall have abundance."[3] In the end, it's all God's money anyway! You and I are simply short-term bookkeepers of our master's money. We're tasked to be good stewards over the assets we are given. These assets include not only our money but also our time, our energy, our presence, our impact, and, of course, our unique and individual talents.

What will you do with yours?

CHAPTER 10

A Case for Creativity

Get paid for using your brain instead of your hands.

—RON LEGRAND

In the previous chapter, you learned the cost-effective methods of real estate investing, like wholesaling and novation, which allow you to profit without ever owning real estate. You also learned the mechanics of creative finance: owner financing, subject to, and lease purchase. In this chapter, I'm sharing the personal lessons, both financial and spiritual, I've gained by using each of these strategies.

In Luke 16:1–13, Jesus offers his disciples a parable of a dishonest manager. "A rich man hired an accountant to handle his affairs, but soon a rumor went around that the accountant was thoroughly dishonest."[1] The rich man confronted the accountant and said, "Get your report in order, for you are to be dismissed."[2] Knowing he would soon be out of work, the accountant made some shrewd deals behind his master's back by reducing the debt owed by several of the master's debtors in exchange for shelter when he is eventually put out. "The rich man had to admire the rascal for being so shrewd. And it is true that the citizens of this world are more clever in dishonesty than the godly are."[3]

"For unless you are honest in small matters, you won't be in large ones."[4] For neither you nor anyone else can serve two masters. You cannot serve both God and money. The pharisees, who dearly loved their money, naturally scoffed at all this.[5]

This parable warns us that if we can't be trusted with worldly wealth, how can we be trusted with true kingdom wealth? How we do one thing is how we do everything. I saw how I was the pharisee Jesus was referring to in Luke 16:14. After doubling my real estate portfolio in one year and making more money than I ever had, it still wasn't enough. I wanted more! I was buying investment properties but selling my soul by giving in to greed.

On Sunday morning at church, I looked like a Christian. But I was living like hell Monday through Friday. I knew I had to get my report in order. If I didn't, I wouldn't have a home—or at least, not a hopeful home—when I am dismissed from this body.

God began showing up in my life through my real estate business. I found Him through my failed endeavors of people and property. He stepped into the mess of my life and helped me create a message for those looking to discover financial freedom while, at the same time, valuing people over property.

Thankfully, I didn't have to have my report in order because Jesus met me where I was—a sinner who was consumed with greed. I was more clever in dishonesty than I was in godly matters. Even after giving my life to Jesus, I would still see how much I could get out of people. After all, this is a business, not a charity.

I'm now learning this real estate business doesn't have to be a zero-sum game. My win doesn't have to come at another's loss. Instead of cleverly trying to deceive people, I can use my creativity to do good, honest work that makes a difference in people's lives. But it wasn't always this way. The case studies below are but just a few of my fumbles. I've categorized them into two segments: active income and passive income strategies.

ACTIVE INCOME: TRADING TIME TODAY FOR CASH TOMORROW

ACTIVE INCOME: FIX AND FLIP

I personally never graduated to the fix and flip model. You already heard how I blundered through my fifth rental property, which caused so much undue stress on me, my money, and my marriage. This BRRR method discussed in chapter eight taught me to buy, rehab, refinance, and rent, but *never* repeat! It was truly swapping one full-time job for another. An investor friend I met at a recent house-flipping mastermind said it best: "When you become a house flipper, you quit your nine-to-five job to work 5:00 a.m. to 9:00 p.m."

Nevertheless, if you enjoy working with your hands and are skilled in the trades, it can be a very lucrative profession. My mentor, Jeff Kemmer, has been flipping houses for decades and does very well. But he warns newer investors: "The fix and flip business is a license to lose money. The most money is at stake, and the risks are the greatest compared to any other strategy. Be prepared to pay the highest tuition if you enroll in the School of Hard Knocks by doing it on your own."

Enough said.

ACTIVE INCOME: WHOLESALING

It took six months of trying and failing to finally land my first local wholesale deal in San Antonio, Texas. In fact, it came to me on the very same day I had given up. I had just turned off my marketing systems and fired my virtual assistant earlier that day. That night, I received a response from one of my social media posts.

"I'm getting divorced and need to sell ASAP," a woman responded.

She wasn't shy about sharing her entire life story with me in a single post. I met her at the house the next day. The house needed a full gut job. We agreed on a purchase price that would give her just enough to move into a new apartment. We signed a contract, and I agreed to pay all her closing costs. After signing the contract, I contacted the same investor-friendly realtor who'd helped me purchase my fourth and fifth properties. My realtor found an investor in his network who was willing to take on the extensive rehab.

Within three weeks, we'd closed the transaction, and I walked away with $24,000!

The day after closing, the seller messaged me, "What are escrow fees?"

"Oh. That's what the title company charges for their work."

"Why does it show I was charged $1,500 for escrow fees? I thought you were going to pay all the closing costs."

Apparently, the title company made an error and charged her these escrow fees instead of the end buyer. Clever in my dishonesty, I quickly devised a story in my head of why she was supposed to pay these fees. I was making a deal behind my master's back, just like the dishonest manager in Jesus's parable.

After crafting my perfectly fabricated story, I was about to hit *send* when my conscience finally caught up. *I just profited $24,000. I think I can afford to do what is right.* The next morning, I met the seller for coffee and cut her a check for $1,500. Though I wasn't walking in faith at this time, God was beginning His work in me *through* my business.

ACTIVE INCOME: NOVATION

My first novation was in South Carolina, and it was the smoothest transaction I'd ever done. The seller had already moved out of state. The house sat vacant for six months. In short, he was done with this property. I mailed a lock box to his neighbor, who placed it on the front door of the property.

I used a flat-fee broker service to get it listed on the local MLS. The property needed work, but I wasn't ready for an out-of-state rehab project. So, I listed it as-is. I knew my buyer pool would be limited, but at the time I didn't have the desire nor the money to invest in a fixer-upper in small-town South Carolina.

Five weeks and fifteen phone calls later, I spoke with a real estate agent who was looking for a home for his younger friend. The house was perfect for this young man. The only problem is that the house would never qualify for a bank loan. The agent really wanted to help his young friend, so he purchased the property all cash and created a seller-finance note with his friend.

My second novation deal didn't go as smoothly, but the numbers were so good I couldn't let it go. My initial profit potential was estimated at $100,000! I tried to leverage every tool I had in my toolbelt: wholesale, fix and flip, sub2, owner finance, cash, and BRRRR.

Note: The more tools you have in your strategy belt, the better manager of worldly wealth you become.

The seller was facing foreclosure. So, purchasing the property subject to the loan staying in the seller's name was out of the question. Within a few months, there would be no loan to assume! The seller was emotionally disconnected from the property. He needed to move down south ASAP and was just going to let the bank foreclose on the house. His asking price equaled his loan balance plus some moving expenses.

The property was in the Great Smoky Mountains of North Carolina with beautiful views—perfect for an Airbnb. There was so much interest in the property because the supply of homes was limited in this area. A realtor responded to my social media post, "I have a cash buyer who will pay your full asking price."

I thought I'd hit the jackpot... until I discovered the house was a mobile home the seller turned into an exotic zoo! He had snakes, iguanas, tarantulas, and seven large dogs. It smelled so bad the realtor couldn't even finish her initial walk-through.

"I'm sorry. But my client is not interested."

In a defeated tone, I called the seller and admitted, "Mr. Seller, I'm sorry, but I am not your buyer. However, I'm still able to assist you."

"How?"

"I can still ensure you get your asking price. But it would require that we list your property to find an investor cash buyer."

"Can't I just do that myself?"

"Yes. You certainly can. But you will have to pay all the closing costs and realtor agent commissions."

"I don't have any money to pay that."

"I'm willing to pay these expenses if you're still open to working with me."

"Yes. Let's do it!"

We eventually landed on a novation agreement.

I asked a local attorney if we could execute this deal in two separate transactions: one between the seller and me and another between myself and the buyer. That way, my profit remained private, and the buyer and the seller would be none the wiser. A clever yet dishonest move. The attorney saw right through my deceitful ways and declined my request.

Remember from chapter nine that in a novation transaction, there is one contract: *everyone* sees *everything*. In this case, it backfired. The buyer's agent saw the seller was only walking away with $3,500. Both the buyer and the seller learned I would receive $21,500. *Oof!*

I began to think, *Why is this happening to me?*

You see, all of this occurred around the same time I began my walk in faith. I was trying to mirror Christ in my personal life, yet the reflection of my business behavior was the complete opposite. It's one thing to be Christian; it's another to be like Christ. That next morning during my prayer time, the question of *Why is this happening to me* came to me again— but in an alternative way: *Why is this happening* for *me? Perhaps God is working on me, so He can eventually do His work* through *me*.

Yes!

In an effort to save the deal, I gave the seller an extra $5,000 at closing and offered the buyer a $5,000 discount. I lost $10,000, but I saved the deal.

With fix and flip, wholesaling, and novation, you're actively working today in hopes of tomorrow's payday. What if there was a better way? Why not perform work today that will pay you tomorrow, next month, next year, and even five or ten years from now? The stories below highlight how you can put in the same work now and create a steady stream of passive income in the future.

PASSIVE INCOME: TRADING CREATIVITY TODAY FOR CONSISTENT CASH FLOW

PASSIVE INCOME: OWNER FINANCE

Earlier this year, I purchased a fixer-upper home in South Carolina that the seller owned free and clear. There was no underlying mortgage. The seller's circumstance met all the criteria from table 3.1 in chapter three. She'd already moved out of state and had a friend staying there, so it wouldn't sit vacant. We signed an owner-finance contract and had our attorney work up a mortgage note. She became the bank, and I became the borrower.

I was willing to accept her higher asking price if she was willing to accept my terms. We agreed on a zero down payment, zero percent interest, and $300 a month for the next fifteen years. The market rent in the area was $1,200 a month, thus creating a cash flow spread of $900 a month until my tenant-buyer obtains his own bank financing.

I hire a local home inspector to assess the condition of every property. In the past, I would knowingly withhold some of the home's hidden defects from my tenant-buyer. I'd let them figure it out. This property over people move was not only dishonest, it also dishonors the partnership I seek to establish with my tenant-buyers.

It doesn't matter what condition the property is in. Once you offer a home as "rent to own, no bank qualifying," people will come out of the woodwork and jump at the opportunity because three out of ten people in America cannot qualify for a mortgage.

But this property needed extensive work. The right tenant-buyer must have vision as well as the skill to perform the repairs. I've made the mistake before of allowing a young couple with no construction experience to take on a similar fixer-upper project. The rehab consumed them financially, and they couldn't keep up. These days, I'm more deliberate in selecting the right partnership.

Within thirty days, a buyer prospect responded to my social media post. He was a general contractor and saw the property's potential. It was perfect for his growing family. Within a month, he had replaced the flooring and patched the sheetrock. He paid $4,000 as a down payment. The deal cost me a total of $2,000 (I spent $500 in advertising expenses plus $1,500 in closing costs). Thus, from day one, I acquired this property for free with $900 a month cash flow!

My friend, Jesse Mills, says it's our job to match up people who can't (distressed sellers) with people who can (eager tenant-buyers). This is a phenomenal way to manage your talents!

PASSIVE INCOME: SUBJECT TO

Two years ago, I closed a property in Louisville, Kentucky, subject to the loan staying in the seller's name. I had to pony up $10,000 to purchase, which was more than I would have preferred. But the deal was too good to let go. The seller had a sick mother in one state and a sick father-in-law in another. The $10,000 would be used to purchase a trailer to travel between his two families. I tried to get the seller to accept $5,000 down. He wouldn't budge. He needed $10,000 for his trailer. If I wanted the deal, I needed to come up with $10,000.

I was willing to give the seller what he wanted for several reasons:

1. The seller's loan had a 3 percent interest rate.
2. The loan was in forbearance. He didn't have to make a payment for another six months. At the end of six months, the lender would add all of his missed payments to the backend loan—no catch-up payments needed.
3. I knew if the seller could walk away with a win, he would be a better long-term partner.
4. My tenant-buyer's down payment was $7,500; the market rent was $2,200; and the seller's mortgage payment was $1,100.

So, in less than six months, I received all my money back. The seller bought his trailer, my tenant-buyer bought the home of her dreams, and I bought a free asset.

PASSIVE INCOME: LEASE PURCHASE

These days, my go-to strategy is the subject to purchase arrangement discussed above because the title transfers out of the seller's name. I control the property. But in my most recent sandwich lease option deal, the seller not only had a mortgage loan, he also had a second lien of $35,000 that had to be paid in full when the title transferred to a new owner. So, sub2 was out of the question.

The seller had been renting out the property, but his tenant fell on hard times and stopped paying the rent five months prior. He couldn't afford to pay two mortgages, nor could he bear the cost of an eviction attorney. I explained I could pay to remove his nonperforming tenant and stop the bleeding. The seller was thrilled!

"I don't need to make any money on this. I just want her out!" he exclaimed.

I contacted the seller's tenant and kindly advised her I would be purchasing the property. As you can imagine, she was not happy. I explained she had thirty days to find a new place to live. I offered cash for keys, as explained in chapter five and six, so the tenant wouldn't have an eviction on her record. I was either going to pay $1,000 to an attorney or to the seller's tenant. But she insisted I must evict her.

It took sixty days to eventually get a court date and another thirty days to get her out. Meanwhile, I kept my promise and continued to pay the seller's mortgage. After the seller's tenant finally moved out, I followed up with my tenant-buyers and began the showings. Within a week, the tenant-buyer and I signed a contract. The down payment was $10,000, and the monthly spread between what I owed the seller's mortgage company and what my tenant-buyer paid me was $1,000 a month. I plan to hold this deal for the next five years or more.

The total time I spent talking with the seller, the attorneys, the seller's tenant, and my tenant-buyer prospects was about forty hours over a six-month period. When I worked in corporate America, I earned an average of $1,000 a week. Now, for the next five years, I will earn $1,000 a month from the forty hours I spent this year. That's leveraging time in your favor.

GETTING YOUR REPORT IN ORDER

Table 10.1. below depicts the profit potential of each deal structure we discussed. This is not to say you couldn't make more in a wholesale deal than you would in a novation or that sub2 will always yield the highest profit. This graph merely represents my personal experience.

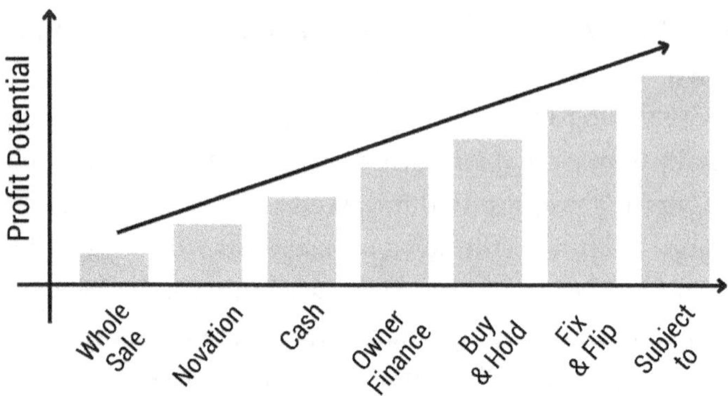

In wholesaling and novation, you invest a large amount of time and only get paid once—then you're dismissed and must find another job. With fix and flip, you invest a significant amount of cash and time—and still only get paid once. With buy and hold, you're required to put a 20 percent down payment, or 100 percent down if you're using cash, but at least you get paid consistently on a monthly basis. Meanwhile, your money remains buried in the deal.

Conversely, with owner finance, sub2, and lease purchase, the same time and effort you invest today offers a payday tomorrow (a down payment from your tenant-buyer), a consistent payday each month (the spread between what you owe the seller and what your tenant-buyer pays you), and a backend payday (when your tenant-buyer qualifies for their own loan and purchases the property).

Table 10.2 represents your return on your invested time. Each deal structure takes time: time to learn; time to implement; time to find a deal; time to nurture seller leads; time to find funding; time to rehab; time to advertise; time to screen tenant-buyers. You have to decide how best you want to leverage the fleeting time you have left on this earth. What is your time worth?

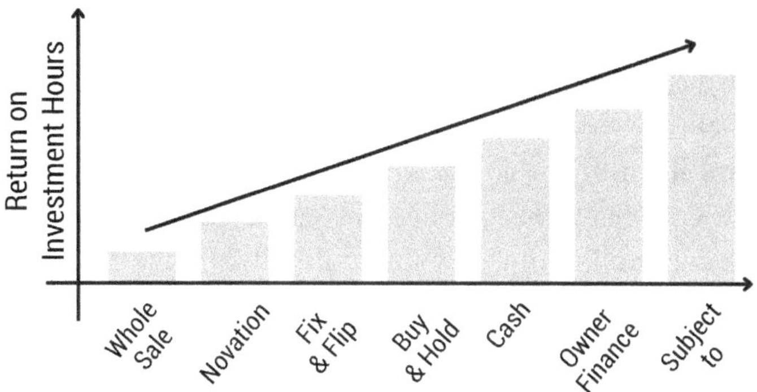

As with everything in life, there is a tradeoff: greater rewards come with greater risks.

Table 10.3 displays the amount of risks inherent in each strategy. Please remember this is only my opinion and shouldn't be construed as fact. There are too many risks to enumerate in this simple bar graph. With any strategy, you may face litigation if you spend more time being clever in dishonesty like the dishonest manager.

At least with wholesaling and novation, the onus is not on you because there is no ownership in the deal. I believe fix and flip is riskier than cash because of the significant amount of work required coupled with the variability of the market. Will your fix and flip project appraise at the estimated price? Will your contractors finish on time or run off with your money?

Subject to is shown as the highest level of risk because the seller's lender *may* call the loan due if they discover the seller no longer holds title to the property (i.e., the lender requires the entire loan balance be paid in full immediately). If this should ever occur, take Robert Paschal's advice when talking to the seller's mortgage company. "Look at the payment history from the time the title transferred and now. Challenge them that calling a loan due that is *performing* goes against their company's mission to drive return."[6] If the lender calls the loan due, you either refinance or place the deed to the property back in the seller's name. In all my years of investing, this has never happened.

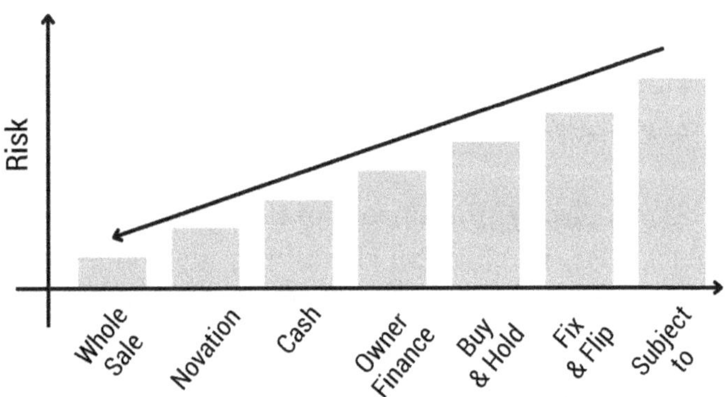

MASTERING YOUR TALENTS

Remember, there is no one *right* strategy. It's a factor of how you use your talents: time, money, skill, drive, determination, impact, influence, and abilities. "You must stop spending your thoughts, your time, and your money. Everything in life must be an investment."[7] We either trade hours for dollars or invest time in people and property to build worldly wealth (ethically, of course) and use it to serve others—thus creating kingdom wealth. Affluence is for influence. Income is for impact.

How will you get your report in order before being dismissed?

Don't be like me by giving in to greed and risk selling your soul by making similar property over people moves. Learn from my mistakes. People are not transactions or tasks that we check off a to-do list. People, relationships, and time are all assets. Property is simply a vehicle in which we become better stewards of our talents. The more we consult God in our business endeavors, the more He blesses us and the people around us.

The parable of the talents in Matthew 25 concludes by saying, "You've been faithful over this small amount, so now I will give you much more."[8] For the man who uses well what he is given shall be given more, and he shall have abundance.[9]

I tried to make my case for creativity clear and concise. Using these strategies, you can cocreate abundance.

SECTION FOUR:

PROSPERITY

CHAPTER 11

The Best Steward of People

No one would remember the Good Samaritan if he'd only had good intentions—he had money as well.[1]

—MARGRET THATCHER

In Luke 10: 30–37, we read Jesus's parable of the Good Samaritan. A man was traveling out of Jerusalem when he was attacked by bandits and was left to die. A local priest and a temple assistant saw him lying there but then went on. A despised man from a rival town of Samaria saw this injured man, covered his wounds, carried him on his donkey, and stayed with him throughout the night. In the morning, the Samaritan paid the local innkeeper to care for the injured man. "If his bill runs higher than that, I'll pay the difference next time I'm here."[2]

Question: Did the Good Samaritan have empathy or compassion?

Empathy says, *What is the emotion of the other person sitting across from me? Let me match that; therefore, we're now in it together.* The challenge this creates is we now have two "stuck" people instead of one. Compassion, on the other hand, recognizes the state the other person is experiencing. They listen to the song the other person is singing but deliberately choose not to become part of that symphony.[3] The compassionate person recognizes this happened and then asks: What can we do with it now? What's the next right move?

I believe the Good Samaritan had compassion. He helped the injured man when others wouldn't. But he didn't stay with the injured man until he recovered fully. Rather, he left him with the innkeeper. He couldn't carry his load forever. Instead, the Good Samaritan helped where he could then continued about his intended business.

The Bible is a living book about relationships. Relationships are the fuel of life.[4] As we discussed in chapter three, the real estate business is a people business. God tasks us to be good stewards of our assets. Assets, in my opinion, extend far beyond tangible goods such as money and property. They also include people and relationships. So, while property appears to be the asset, we, as investors, must remember it is the people we serve that hold the highest value.

As investors, we are intimately involved in people's lives. We may know more about them than most of their friends. A seller may not tell his family he's facing foreclosure, but he tells you. A tenant-buyer may not tell her spouse she lost her job, but she tells you.

We're not only investing for income. We're also investing in people's outcomes.

Looking back now to when I first began investing, I could see how I was the bandit in the night that attacked an innocent man—not physically, but deceitfully through stretching the truth and squeezing people for my own selfish gain. I'd rationalize my behavior by telling myself, "The seller agreed to it," or, "They knew their down payment was nonrefundable."

THE BEST STEWARD OF PEOPLE

The parable of the talents covered in chapters nine and ten advised we are to be good stewards of property. We are also tasked with being good stewards of people. We do this by helping people *through* property: sellers who need *out* and buyers who want *in*.

Author John Townsend had this to say about a steward: "A steward is an administrator, or director, of people or property. Stewardship is about responsibility. He can be responsible for the care and maintenance of a Fortune 500 company, a garden, or a family. The buck stops with the steward."[5]

Pastor Jim Baker notes, "A steward in the New Testament times was a person who managed someone else's property, finances, or other affairs and were not the owner of the property they managed."[6]

Our name is on God's account. We have unrestricted access to it. If we think like owners, we are abusing that privilege. When we think like stewards or investment managers, we always look for the best place to invest our owner's money.[7] Being a good steward of our talents means serving those in our business.

A steward who maintains a people over property mindset leverages their talent to leave people better off than where they found them, just like the Good Samaritan.

What this looks like for sellers is by:

- Introducing a seller who is facing foreclosure to a credit repair company.
- Connecting a seller to another investment company that could provide them with a better solution.
- Informing the seller they can get more money by listing the property with a local real estate agent.
- Taking on the burden of a squatting tenant.

What this looks like for tenant-buyers is by:

- Helping them enroll in a credit repair program.
- Cheering them on about the progress they're making with the property repairs.
- Being a good reference for them for their new job.
- Treating them like an owner and speaking as if they've already purchased the property.

For sellers worried about their credit score, inform them their credit will improve as you make their mortgage payment for them. For both seller and tenant-buyers, find ways to give them a win. There's no need to use every strong-arm negotiation tactic in the book and walk away on top every time. They're not your enemy. They're your partner. Treat them like one.

Our work is about people, not indirectly but directly and in all aspects. It is performed with people, done by people, and for people. There is no work, as we understand it, without people.[8] God has always desired to be at the center of His people. God is pro-relationship and is anti-isolation. Relationships are seen as crucial in the Bible. In John 15:1–5, Jesus pictured his attachment to us as a vine and the branches.[9]

> I am the true Vine and my Father is the Gardener. He lops off every branch that doesn't produce. And he prunes those branches that bear fruit for even larger crops. He has already tended you by pruning you back for greater strength and usefulness by means of the commands I gave you. Take care to live in me, and let me live in you. For a branch cannot produce fruit when severed from the vine. Nor can you be fruitful apart from me. Yes, I am the Vine; you are the branches. Whoever lives in me and I in him shall produce a large crop of fruit. For apart from me you can't do a thing.[10]

This passage instructs us to be connected to Him and connected to His people. I created a Connectivity Checklist that sits on my desk to ensure I remain connected to people I encounter. I ask myself these questions when I talk to a seller or tenant-buyer, evaluate a deal, or draft a contract.

- Would God bless this agreement?
- What if my friends and family knew I was doing this?
- How can I help this person find a win?
- Does my solution serve this person? Or just me?
- Is *my* solution the best possible solution?
- Would this person be better suited going with another company?
- How can I help this person even if we don't do this deal?

This connectivity checklist reminds me there's another person on the other end of the phone who needs help. If you focus on the needs of the people, you will be able to find better deals because you are finding ways to create win-wins and not taking advantage of people.

THE BEST INVESTOR YOU'LL EVER MEET

There are many real estate experts out there. I have learned from many of them. But the best investor I've met so far has been Jesus. You probably never thought of Jesus as an investment guru. But he is. He took twelve misfits and turned them into assets. He managed to take five loaves of bread and two fish and fed five thousand people! He taught his students to love people versus exploiting them and advised them to seek Him by investing in the poor.

The dividends of His love are automatically reinvested when we carry that love forward to His people. The long-term capital gain that His love creates is tax-deferred and can be written off each time we confess or repent. He is not only a private lender but also a certified people accountant.

Jesus is the trustee of the largest portfolio in the world, with assets under management valued at over 2.5 billion people alive today, the largest holdings of any fiduciary ever! Jesus empowers His missionaries to enter into unknown markets and make blind offers of faith to its residents. The interest rate he charges for His services is unlike any other investor. If we commit to following His word, our days on the market are the best in the industry.

The return on invested capital we yield when we put our faith in him becomes infinite. The thirty-plus years He invested on earth has never depreciated, even after two thousand years, making the loan amortization period eternal. He issues us a line of credit that remains open to anyone who is willing to believe in Him.

We can never go spiritually bankrupt if we believe in Him— even if that means we lose everything we *think* we own on our balance sheet. He's already paid our closing costs in advance. The only concession He asked for is our faith and trust. He's performed his own competitive market analysis and determined our after repair value will continue to appraise higher and higher the more we spend time in His word.

His loan to value exceeds that of any other lender in the marketplace today. Jesus bought us on a short sale. Our lives before Him didn't equal the loan balance that God issued us before the fall of Adam and Eve. Yet, we passed His underwriting criteria, and He paid the full asking price when He bought us with his blood. Jesus used his own life as a down payment assistance program to help His people get into the eternal home of their dreams.

Our lives become fully funded the moment we give our lives to Him, and he didn't ask for a commission. When we reach the end of our lives, we will sit across from Jesus at the closing table. The only assignment fee He'll ask for is how we served Him by serving His people.

When you think about it, why wouldn't you want to partner with an investor who can multiply everything in your life?

GIVING

For decades, my relationship with money has been in constant flux. Growing up, I heard "money is the root of all evil." I always wanted a lot of money, but apparently God didn't want that. I always settled for just enough. After all, shouldn't our daily bread be sufficient? I mistakenly believed that to satisfy God, I must accept a meager salary, give away what little money I had, and let people walk all over me.

Now, as I've gotten to spend more time in my Bible, I learned it's not money that's the issue; rather, it's the love of money that is the root of all evil.[11] The Bible has more than 2,300 verses that deal with money. Jesus talks about money in eleven of his thirty-nine parables. This topic matters to God.[12] Isn't it ironic the whole world belongs to God, yet so often we don't bother to ask Him how he wants us to invest, give, spend, and save?[13]

The more I researched, the more I saw how much God wants us to prosper. My friend Sophia told me it is God's will for us to prosper in life as long as we keep Him first. Money only becomes the root of all evil when you put money and greed before God. God should be our first love.

In an interview with Nick Spohn, he suggested that money is a tool to live an enriched life and to bless others. Money isn't good or bad. It's our intentions or judgments of it that make it so. We are supposed to be a pipeline for God's riches, not a vault.

God's going to want to know what we did for the least of these. What we do with what God gives us is the test. He's going to want to see what we did with the talents He gave us.[14] We say we trust in God. But too often, our actions reveal what we really trust is our bank accounts. Our heart is revealed by the way we treat money.[15] Giving, by definition, releases control.[16]

We'll never reach this world with our spare time and our spare change. Give radically! But we mustn't fool ourselves. If we're not willing to give $1 when we have $10, we're not going to give $1,000 when we have $10,000. You can give without loving, but you cannot love without giving.[17] God loves a cheerful giver.[18]

How do we ensure money doesn't have an unnecessary influence over us? The very best place to start is by prioritizing people.[19] Generosity is our currency! All the things we love have people behind them.

Jesus made it clear we are to help the poor. And the poorest way to help the poor is to be poor.[20] Prosperity can be measured in how much we give away because nothing on this earth is ours anyway. We must steward what we have before we can increase it more. Let's use our money to help people versus using people to help our money.

Being a good steward of people means using your talents to serve others. Your talents extend far beyond what's in your wallet. Your talent includes your time, your presence, your ability, your availability, your wit, your personality, your insight, your knowledge, your skill, and your smile. Make a decision to give some of your talents wherever you go, to whomever you see. As long as you're giving, you will be receiving.[21]

Pastor Jim Baker noted, "Prosperity has a purpose. True prosperity is not about toys and trinkets. It's about influence and impact. Affluence is for influence. Income is for impact." All this prosperity is available if you're willing to serve God and His people. Service is the price we pay for our space on Earth.

The late Kobe Bryant said it best: "It's not about you, man… get over yourself."[22]

CHAPTER 12

Time and Mind Freedom

You can stop working now, Dad. We already have enough money. How much more do we need?

—MY SIX-YEAR-OLD DAUGHTER

Hearing my daughter say these words hurt my heart. She'd just come home from school and was excited to play. My normal response when she comes into my office is, "Daddy has to work so we can have money."

Real estate investing has become my passion. It doesn't feel like work anymore. Left unchecked, I could easily work all day and night. I'm teaching my daughter about money and how it can be used to provide for our family and others. But her statement above proved I still have a lot to learn about wealth and prosperity. Thankfully, our children come through us to teach us our greatest lessons. In my daughter's eyes, it doesn't matter how much money I make. All she wants is time. To kids, love is time. The higher the quantity, the higher the quality.[1]

God called us to work. It's how we express ourselves creatively. Business is God's arrangement. Human beings didn't think it up. We put some variation on it, but it is a part of God's design, by which human beings love and serve one another.[2] I believed my work life was my real life, or at least the means to a real life. Constant tension existed between real life and work.[3] I still struggle with this today. It may look like I'm resting because I'm away from my computer, but in my head, I'm still working. I am physically present with family while mentally consumed with work.

More recently, as I let go of the poisons of alcohol and smoking, I began filling that void with work—replacing one addiction (drugs) for another (work) and putting property over people (family). *If I just get this next property, then I'll have enough money*, I thought. Peace of mind eluded me because I was never present in the moment. And it didn't matter how many more properties I acquired. If what I have now isn't enough, it'll never be enough. God never intended our jobs to push the rest of our lives out of balance. Our goal should be to plan work around our lifestyles. But, I fell into the trap of planning my lifestyle around my work. Yikes!

But money is not the measure of our value of work in God's eyes. The most important thing you bring home from work is not a paycheck. It's you, your spirit, your integrity of heart.

The importance of rest is evident throughout the Old and New Testament. Genesis 2:3 states, "And God blessed the seventh day and declared it holy because it was the day when he ceased this work of creation." Mark 2:27 says, "Sabbath was made for the benefit of man, and not man to benefit the

Sabbath." God can do more in six days than man can do in seven. If the All-mighty requires rest, so do we.

If our lives do not have an off switch, then we can never turn on when it's our time to shine. We need constant reinforcement that the world does not revolve around you or me or depend upon our labor. Even the sun doesn't come out every day. God calls us to burn up in service—not burn out.[4] In his book, *The Sabbath*, Abraham Joshua Herschel concludes, "The higher goal of spiritual living is not to amass a wealth of information but to face sacred moments. Sabbath is not a reward for hard work. Sabbath is a gift that precedes work and enables us to work. Rest is never a reward. It's a gift."[5]

We all need a day to simply rest.

A DAY OR TWO OF REST

I began investing in real estate six years ago with the goal of retiring my wife, Lynn, which we accomplished in less than two years. Retiring me, however, wasn't as clear. I knew I wanted to leave corporate America—I just didn't know how or when.

On Monday morning, March 15, 2021, I finally had enough! Though I didn't quit that exact day, I knew I'd reached my limit and the end was near. My eyes glazed over hundreds of new and unanswered emails awaiting my reply. I'd become the single point of contact for every decision in my department. No one wanted to make a decision because no one wanted to make the wrong one. Admittedly, I enjoyed the ego stroke of the pseudo control I thought I had; therefore, I refused to delegate.

But too many requests from too many directions became an incredible burden on me. Cross-departmental projects needed my attention. I had several pet projects I was pursuing, not to mention projects assigned by the department executives, and *none* of them were getting done! For the better part of six months, my only job was answering emails! Thus, fifty projects were going on simultaneously, and *I* was the bottleneck. Argh!

I begrudgingly began answering emails—at least, I tried. I read the first email. *Nope, I'm not answering that. Nuh-uh, I'm not answering that one either.* I sat back in my chair and thought, *I really don't feel like doing this today.* I ran downstairs and found Lynn sitting at the kitchen table.

"Do you want to go to the beach today?" I asked.

"Absolutely!" she exclaimed.

I raced back upstairs, canceled my meetings, packed up the gear, and scurried off to the beach. We had an amazing time building sandcastles, swimming in the ocean, and walking along the shoreline. It was so much fun I didn't want to leave! *Could I afford to ditch work one more day?* I wondered. Why not? I've already gone this far. We booked a hotel for the night and played another day. But all good things must come to an end.

Wednesday morning, back in my home office, I looked at my inbox of even *more* new and unanswered emails and concluded, "I don't feel like working today either!" I obviously couldn't keep up my ditch day strategy without getting fired. I slammed my laptop shut and met my wife at the kitchen table once again.

"You remember how we said I'd quit my job in the next year or two?"

"Yes..."

"Instead of waiting, what if I put in my ninety-day notice right now?"

I tensed up, held my breath, and waited for the worst. We both knew we weren't financially ready. But Lynn, being the supportive and faithful wife she is, said, "Go for it—God will provide." Those words were exactly what I needed. Within six months of leaving corporate America, I replaced my active income with passive investment income by using the strategies discussed in the book.

Though money will never make us happy, it can bring us peace.

FINANCIAL PEACE

Real estate investing is a vehicle that can drive your financial freedom, steer you toward time freedom and peace of mind freedom, and help you arrive at a state of peace. The five ways in which real estate can bring you financial PEACE are:

P—Principal paydown
E—Equity capture
A—Appreciation
C—Cash flow
E—Excise benefits (taxes and depreciation)

1. *Principle paydown*

   The tenants pay the mortgage payment. The longer they stay, the lower the loan balance and the larger your equity spread.

2. *Equity capture*

   If you purchase below market value, you are essentially gaining free equity (ownership) in the property. You can also capture equity by making improvements—thus increasing its value in the marketplace.

3. *Appreciation*

   Appreciation is the natural increase in a property's value over time. History has shown that real estate valuations increase over long periods—but not always, not forever, and not at the same rate in every region. However, over the long haul, real estate values rise because of the scarcity of properties.

4. *Cash flow*

   Monthly cash flow is the most immediate and tangible form of profit. It's the reason I got into real estate in the first place. Cash flow is what's paying my bills each month. If I don't feel like working today, I don't have to because cash flow is providing liquidity.

5. *Excise benefits (tax/depreciation)*

The government wants us to own our home as well as other income-producing properties. They prove that by providing a mountain of tax breaks for investors and homeowners. The government also understands that houses lose their usability as time passes. You can write off this devaluation over 27.5 years for single-family homes in the US, thus reducing your tax bill each year by a specified amount just for owning property. On top of that, you can write off the mortgage interest paid throughout the year. The more properties you own, the further you reduce your tax obligation.

BONUS BENEFIT: LEVERAGE

An added bonus you receive with real estate investing is this concept of leverage. When you purchase below market value, there is unrealized equity sitting in the property. If your strategy is to hold on to the property, you can borrow against that equity to obtain a new mortgage loan for your next investment property—increasing your monthly cash flow. When you buy real estate, you're building leverage for yourself and your business. Caution—leverage magnifies your gains and also amplifies losses if property values decline. If this occurs, your losses will be substantially larger when you use leverage. So, *leverage* this lever lightly!

I hope you see why 90 percent of all millionaires earned their wealth through real estate investing. Where else can you get paid in five different ways? Once you establish financial peace, it's crucial to create a plan that protects your priorities. We do this by leveraging other people's time.

DELEGATION

Work is about people, not indirectly but directly and in all aspects. It is performed with people, done by people, and for people. There is no work, as we understand it, without people.[6] For years, I've fallen into the trap of *No one can run my business as good as me!* Consequently, that mentality ensured I'd always be working *for* my business. If I didn't work that day, the task would be waiting for me the next day. I fooled myself into thinking I was free. Meanwhile, I performed all the $5 to $15 per hour tasks, which is the exact opposite of time freedom!

That's when my colleague, Sean, reminded me, "The more you continue to do it all, the more you block someone else's blessing." While no one can do it better than me, a lot more people can do a lot more than I can alone. Admittedly, the people I finally hired are doing my work better, faster, and cheaper.

As business owners, we work *on* the business and find competent people to work *in* the business. Now, I'm watching my team work on tasks I thought would always be mine. Time freedom is not just about how much time you spend doing what you love. It's also how little time you spend doing what you hate.[7] When we invest in others to perform our work, we're not only investing in them, we're also investing in our future time freedom.

REDEFINING PROSPERITY

True prosperity is more than just money. Money will never define how wealthy I am. At a recent conference in Austin, Texas, Mel Abraham said that legacy isn't something we leave *behind* for someone. It's something we leave *within* someone in the moments of interaction we have with them. He challenged his audience to stop measuring wealth in dollars and instead measure it in time. Dollars in the bank might stroke our ego and allow us to take nice vacations. But prosperity—to me—embodies so much more. It's multidimensional: physical, mental, emotional, intellectual, relational, and spiritual, both in the personal and professional setting.

The definition of prosperity has taken on new meaning as I grow older—both in age and in my faith. I always thought to be prosperous meant to be rich, which it does. However, my only gauge of prosperity was money. Nowadays, I have a broader view of wealth. To be rich and wealthy means to be happy with where I am in my journey; to be present in the task in front of me; to feel connected to God; to have both time freedom and peace of mind freedom; to enjoy the work I choose to engage in; to have love and be loved by others; to know I am aligned to what I seek and to progress along my chosen path; to strive; to grow; to desire and pursue despite failure or doubt.

Pastor Ed Newton gave an amazing talk recently about the subject of money and what it can and cannot provide:

> Money can buy you a bed. But it can't buy you rest. It can buy you a smartphone, but it can't give you smarts. It can buy you fine foods, but it can't buy you satisfaction. It buys you name brands, but it can't buy you worth; plastic surgery, not beauty; a house, but not a home; medicine, not healing; luxury, not legacy; entertainment, not joy; followers, not friends; success, not faithfulness; sex, not love. Money will never be satisfied.

Prosperity is not about generating money to be happy. It's about generating happiness—period! But how can we generate happiness? How could we redefine prosperity? One way I've learned this is through measuring daily progress instead of waiting to be happy *when*…

With progress as the goal, each day I can achieve my outcome, regardless of how many properties I purchase or to-do boxes I check. Whatever I completed that day was enough. I'll never get it all done; yet, there will always be progress! The goalposts will always move further out. As I fulfill one desire, another is born. Therefore, I strive to be satisfied, knowing my day's efforts led to progress.

SO, WHAT DO YOU DO WITH TIME FREEDOM?

We've all been taught to seek financial freedom. But what does that mean? Essentially, it means your lifestyle is financially supported whether you work or not. How I've begun to interpret this is through time and peace of mind. Time freedom means being able to do what I could not do if I had to clock in to work every day. Peace of mind freedom means living life on my own terms and choosing what work will look like, whether it be investing, volunteering, writing a book, creating content, training others, building new businesses, speaking, and so on.

My wife and I were recently reflecting on this idea of time freedom. It's easier to nurture other categories of your life when you're not bound to a nine-to-five job. We can schedule a date day or spend time working on our relationship spiritually, emotionally, and physically.

We contrasted that to where we were five years ago when I was working ten hours a day at the office and bringing home the stresses of work. Why are we so much happier now? One factor is that with more time freedom, you create time to work on what matters most. If your relationships matter, you have the free time to work on improving them.

I've seen people announce their retirement. And within a few short months, they've returned to work! Why is that? It's because that's all they ever knew. What are you naturally inclined to do? For me, I built a real estate business. Well, now that that's sustained, I'm not going to go sit on a beach. Maybe I will for a week or so. But, over time, I'm going to gravitate back to what I'm naturally inclined to do and enjoy doing, which is building a business.

What's your purpose in life?

If you don't know, don't worry, because it's ever-changing. Author Brendon Burchard says we have many purposes throughout our lives. He says your "purpose is found where your interests and passion meet contribution and persistence."[8] What do you enjoy doing on a consistent basis? Where do you feel like you have the greatest ability to contribute to an industry? A cause? A community? Jay Shetty says, "Your passion is for you, and your purpose is for others."

In a discussion with my friend, Ryan, he shared a simple pie chart that may help you find where your true calling may live as you create more time freedom. Ryan told me this is how he found his God-given calling.

FINDING YOUR CALLING

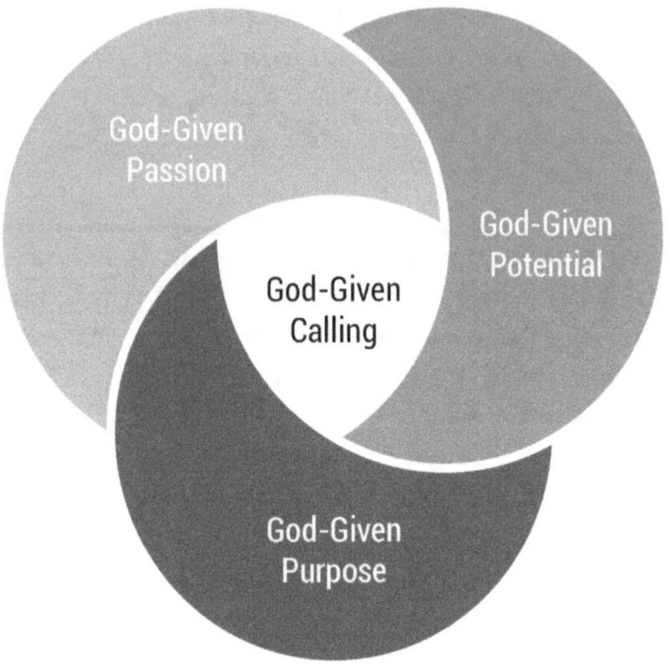

TABLE 11.1 YOUR GOD-GIVEN CALLING

What do you suspect is your God-given calling? Where do your purpose, passion, and potential intersect?

One way to begin brainstorming your God-given calling is to write out your perfect day. I did this when I first began my investing career. I wrote down what life in retirement would look like. What would be my perfect day? Write down what you value most and ensure that time for these items is preserved. As of this writing, my ideal weekday consists of the following:

Wake up refreshed after seven hours of sleep.

3:30 a.m. to 4:30 a.m.:
- Devotion and prayer
- Planning, journaling, and forecasting

4:30 a.m. to 6:30 a.m.:
- Writing

6:30 a.m. to 7:30 a.m.:
- Time with family

7:30 a.m. to 8:30 a.m.:
- Nature walk with my dog

8:30 a.m. to 10:30 a.m.:
- Team meetings
- Build as new business

10:30 a.m. to noon:
- Exercise

Noon to 2:00 p.m.:
- Build new personal and business relationships
- Nurture existing relationships

2:00 p.m. to 3:00 p.m.:
- Nurture new seller and tenant-buyer leads

3:00 p.m. to 5:00 p.m.:
- Seller and tenant-buyer appointments

5:00 p.m. to 7:30 p.m.:
- Time with family

7:30 p.m. to 8:30 p.m.:
- Read before bed

I don't do all these *every* day. I usually sleep in one day a week and typically leave Thursdays and Fridays wide open for creative brainstorming or a date day with my wife. I also aim to volunteer 10 percent of my workweek to causes I am passionate about. Keep in mind this is an *ideal* day. It's something I aim for, but I remain satisfied even if I only accomplish a fraction of these events. I'm not aiming for done because it'll never be done. Instead, what I'm aiming for is progress.

Notice that my ideal day is still filled with work. That's intentional. God has called us to work. But now it's work on my terms; it's work that's aligned with my passion, my purpose, and my potential. There's this myth that once you earn enough passive income, you'll stop working and live on the beach. I've spoken with several investors who've done this. All of them have moved back home within a year.

What does your time freedom look like? How would your peace of mind and freedom play out? Where can your internal passion align with your external purpose?

TIME'S UP

Time—it's the one asset that's always fleeting. No matter how much we invest in it, we can never get it back. So, invest it wisely, friend. If you're only working for a paycheck, you are vastly underpaid. As you free up your calendar and your mental head space, you're more open to finding your God-given calling: the place at which your passion, purpose, and potential intersect. This is where you will find work most meaningful to you. The book you just read was made possible by the time freedom that real estate investing created.

Acquiring investment property gives you financial freedom and time freedom. But only if you consciously make time for rest and delegate activities that do not serve you. With more time, you're more present with the people in your life. The less you have to work, the more time you get to devote to the people in your life.

What I'd been aiming for all along with time freedom was a life on my terms. I wanted to call the shots! But, as I grow deeper in the Word, Jesus is showing me now more than ever that He wants *my* life on *His* terms. The more I align my life on His terms, the more freedom He will provide. And no real estate investment portfolio could provide that type of time or mind freedom!

Invest with God. Invest in His word first. Invest in His work second.[9] Hire Him as your coach, mentor, financial adviser, and accountability partner. He'll show you how to buy investment properties without selling your soul.

Conclusion: People over Property

We began this book with a challenging question: "How does your faith affect the way you invest?"[1]

Our prosperity does not have to come at the expense of other people. We can build a legitimate business, a lifestyle, a legacy, a lifetime stream of income, and honor our Lord by loving His people. But building a people over property portfolio doesn't occur by happenstance. It is done intentionally—strong-rooted in faith and watered frequently.

A people over property portfolio begins with your burning desire to create time freedom by shepherding people through property. Even if your desire is the size of a mustard seed, continue sowing those seeds everywhere you go. But understand that some seeds will fall on rocky ground where the numbers don't work, other seeds will be eaten up by nay-sayers, while other seeds will fall on good soil where you connect your seller's specific circumstance with the right strategy.

As you sow these seeds, remember to be persistent like the friend who came knocking on the door at midnight. He kept knocking until he finally got what he wanted. His persistence paid off, and yours will too! Ask. Seek. Knock. Be persistent in your desire and ask in His name for help. The doors of time freedom and eternal freedom will open. The decision to enter through those doors is yours.

As you knock, you may find a lost sheep—a seller who desperately needs to sell and has lost hope. Are you committed enough to leave the 99 percent and focus 100 percent of your attention on helping the 1 percent who've lost their way? As you talk to God, He will help separate the good wheat from the weeds, and you will find a partner willing to accept your creative solution because it benefits them just as much as it benefits you.

But not every seller or tenant will be a partner, and that's okay. Some may be akin to the workers in the vineyard who plotted to kill the vineyard owner's son and take his crop. Let us not become like the unforgiving servant whose debt was wiped clean, yet he couldn't offer the same grace to his debtors. Choose to forgive sooner those who attempt to take your crop or take advantage of you.

As you sow more seeds and knock on more doors, your talents increase. You become an even better steward of property. You no longer behave like the fearful servant who buried his master's money in the ground. The larger your portfolio, the larger the pool of people you serve.

As your talents grow, you manage more of your master's money. Remember to get your affairs in order and do not behave like the dishonest manager who made shrewd agreements behind his master's back. Choose to be humble in your honesty versus clever in your dishonesty. Great returns come because of biblical values—not at the expense of them. As you faithfully follow the best investor of people, He gives you almost everything you ask for in life… as long as you accept *His* asking price and *His* terms.

A portfolio based on people over property takes work. So, please remember to rest. God can do more in six days than you can in seven. I know you're working hard today to create time and mind freedom. Understand that you can create it now by delegating tasks and letting go of what doesn't serve you. The less you do, the more you will make.[2] I promise!

With more time, you're more present with the people in your life. The less you "have to" work, the more time you get to spend serving the people in your life. This extra time enables your natural gifts to shine and helps you define your God-given calling.

In time, more of your active effort turns into passive income. Yet, that doesn't mean you become passive. Passivity never pays off. You'll still be actively serving others. Your income becomes passive; however, your outcome remains active.

You've reached the end of this book, but your real estate journey has just begun. You decide what you will do from here. What will be your next right move? Will you...

- Attend a real estate meetup group?
- Dedicate one hour a week to educating yourself?
- Connect with a real estate agent to send you deals?
- Invest in a local property yourself?
- Join your local Real Estate Investment Association (REIA)?
- Hire a coach?

Whatever it is, do *something*. Don't let the birds of distraction or busyness swallow this desire. If all you've taken away from this is a few hours of entertainment, I failed. But if this information leads you into action, then mission accomplished.

We can acquire all the properties and possessions we want. But we must understand all our investments, our properties, and our money—even our bodies—aren't ours. We're all God's property. We are simply tenants who are given the option to purchase an eternity with Him. Jesus is the qualified buyer who purchased our souls using his down payment assistance program that's available to all who have faith in Him.

With that understanding, my friend, you can buy investment properties without selling your soul!

Acknowledgments

First, I acknowledge you, the reader, for making it all the way to the end of the book. Thank you.

To my wife, Lynn. Thank you for being my number one fan. I appreciate your extreme patience during this process. I snuck off to bed early so I could wake up early and write. I ducked out on important events to finish chapters. Your grace is what I cherish the most. I love you!

I also extend love and gratitude to all my beta readers and those who gave time and insights, either directly through a one-on-one interview or indirectly in an online survey. Your responses provided clarity in a sea of confusion.

A very special thanks to my friends and family who helped prefund the cost of publishing. You invested in me without knowing if this book was worth buying, which gave me hope in moments where I had none.

Adam Beasley, Alfonso Aramburo, Amy Espinoza, Andres Hernandez, Ashley McCrady, Bernadette Laxamana, Blair

Halver, Cathy Becker, Chasity Henry, CJ Escobedo, Daniel Kohli, Dave Lemke, David Purinton, David Snyder, Dianne Ritter, Dolores Esparza, Donnie Laurence, Edward Lavin, Emily Hammer, Eric Lyman, Eric Morse, Erin Lemke, Fernie Rizo, Forrest James, Frieda Lemke, Gerald Gaenslen, Gillian Lemke, Helen Hunter, Heyli Yero, Ivan Vera, James Bohan, James Shroyer, Janet Bruins, Jason Pucel, Jeff Kemmer, Jesse Almaraz, Jim Horn, Jonathan Geserick, Jose Holguin, Judy Gaenslen, Justin Noethe, Karen Lemke, Kizzie Davis, Lee Currier, Madeline Escobar, Manuel Prado, Melanie Michael, Michael McVerry, Nathan Keeler, Nicholas Galarza, Nona Gomez, Pebby Garner, Philip Revland, Ramya JP, Renee Rendon, Richard Villarreal, Roger Osorio, Ruben Rosas, Ryan Pahler, Sal Scalia, Terri Huber, Tim Allums, TJ Dunn, Tony Beranek, and Vince Scalia

Finally, a special shout out to Eric Koester for creating the Modern Authors Accelerator program. You're right: Anyone can write a book. But not everyone can finish writing a book.

Notes

INTRODUCTION:

1. Keller, Timothy, Andy Crouch, and Cathie Wood, *Faith Driven Investing: Every Investment Has Impact—What's Yours?* (Carol Stream, IL: Tyndale House, 2022), 1.

2. Ibid, 32.

3. Keller, Timothy, Andy Crouch, and Cathie Wood, *Faith Driven Investing: Every Investment Has Impact—What's Yours?* (Carol Stream, IL: Tyndale House, 2022), 88.

4. Ibid, 122.

5. Keller, Timothy, Andy Crouch, and Cathie Wood, *Faith Driven Investing: Every Investment Has Impact—What's Yours?* (Carol Stream, IL: Tyndale House, 2022), 79.

6. Matthew 13:31–32 (The Living Bible)

CHAPTER 1:

1. Goddard, Neville, *Your Faith Is Your Fortune* (New York, NY: Noah Press, 2022), 519.

2. Dryer, Wayne, *Your Sacred Self,* read by the author (HarperAudio, 2005), audio, 2 hours 26 minutes.

3. Matthew 13:1–23 (*The Living Bible*).

4. Cloud, Henry and John Townsend, *Boundaries: When to Say Yes How to Say No to Take Control of Your Life* (Grand Rapids, MI: Zondervan, 2017), 281.

5. Hansen, Brant, *Unoffendable: How Just One Change Can Make All of Life Better* (Nashville, TN: Thomas Nelson, 2023), 199.

6. Luke 11:8 (*The Living Bible*).

7. Matthew 6:6–7 (*The Living Bible*).

8. Mark 11:24 (*The Living Bible*).

9. Goddard, Neville, *Prayer: The Art of Believing* (Grand Rapids, MI: Noah Press, 2022), 221.

10. Ibid, 205.

11. Butts, David, *Forgotten Power: A Simple Theology for a Praying Church* (Sacramento, CA: PrayerShop, 2015), 29.

12. Keller, Timothy, Andy Crouch, and Cathie Wood, *Faith Driven Investing: Every Investment Has Impact—What's Yours?* (Carol Stream, IL: Tyndale House, 2022), 15.

CHAPTER 2:

1. Keller, Gary, *The Millionaire Real Estate Investor* (Columbus, OH: McGraw Hill, 2005), 111.

2. Timothy, Andy Crouch, and Cathie Wood, *Faith Driven Investing: Every Investment Has Impact—What's Yours?* (Carol Steam, IL: Tyndale House, 2022), 70.

3. Ibid, 43–44.

4. John 16:24 (The Living Bible).

5. David Butts, *Forgotten Power: A Simple Theology for a Praying Church* (Sacramento, CA: PrayerShop, 2015), 38

6. Ibid, 29.

7. Goddard, Neville, *Your Faith Is Your Fortune* (New York, NY: Noah Press, 2022), 521.

8. Butts, David, *Forgotten Power: A Simple Theology for a Praying Church* (Sacramento, CA: PrayerShop, 2015), 54.

9. Luke 18:1 (*The Living Bible*).

10. Luke 18:3 (*The Living Bible*).

11. Luke 18:5 (*The Living Bible*).

12. Luke 18:7 (*The Living Bible*).

13. Hansen, Brant, *Unoffendable: How Just One Change Can Make All of Life Better* (Nashville, TN: Thomas Nelson, 2023) 180.

CHAPTER 3:

1. Morby, Pace, *Wealth without Cash: Supercharge Your Real Estate Investing with Subject-To, Seller Financing, and other Creative Deals* (Denver, CO: Bigger Pockets, 2023), 17.

2. Matthew 18:12–13 (*The Living Bible*).

3. Ziglar, Zig, *Secrets of Closing the Sale: For Anyone Who Must Get Others to Say Yes!* (San Francisco, CA: Magna, 2002), 81.

CHAPTER 4:

1. Matthew 13:26 (*The Living Bible*).

2. Morby, Pace, *Wealth without Cash: Supercharge Your Real Estate Investing with Subject-To, Seller Financing, and Other Creative Deals* (Denver, CO: Bigger Pockets, 2023), 120.

3. Ibid, 152.

4. Pucel, Jason, "Religion & Business?" Grace By the Drop, August 1 2023, Educational video, 11:18 to 11:24, https://www.youtube.com/watch?v=ZOeSqKKObho.

5. Keller, Timothy, Andy Crouch, and Cathie Wood, *Faith Driven Investing: Every Investment Has Impact—What's Yours?* (Tyndale House, 2022), 208.

6. Ibid, 70.

CHAPTER 5:

1. Hill, Napoleon, *Success Through a Positive Mental Attitude* (San Antonio, TX: Zinc Read, 2023), 232.
2. Luke 13:7 (*The Living Bible*).
3. Luke 13:8–9 (*The Living Bible*).

CHAPTER 6:

1. Jefferson, Joseph, *Immortality* (New York, NY: Pranava Books, 2022), 5.
2. Cloud, Henry, and John Townsend, *Boundaries: When to Say Yes How to Say No to Take Control of Your Life* (Grand Rapids, MI: Zondervan, 2017, 51).
3. Matthew 18:29 (*The Living Bible*).
4. Matthew 18:32–33 (*The Living Bible*).
5. Matthew 21:41 (*The Living Bible*).
6. Proverbs 16:26 (*The Living Bible*).
7. Galatians 6:5 (*The Living Bible*).
8. 2 Thessalonians 3:10 (*The Living Bible*).
9. Vaynerchuk, Gary, "Why You Should Hire Fast and Fire Faster," GaryVee, June 29, 2023, Educational video, 0:03 to 0:07, https://www.youtube.com/watch?v=-r8zKoNx_YA.

CHAPTER 7:

1. Tew, Robert, *Homeland Enemy Ambush* read by Paul Scott (Red Bank, NJ: Newman Springs Publishing, Inc., 2022), audio, 3 hours 23 minutes.
2. Cloud, Henry, and John Townsend, *Boundaries: When to Say Yes How to Say No to Take Control of Your Life* (Grand Rapids, MI: Zondervan, 2017), 30.
3. Ibid, 171.

4. Cloud, Henry, and John Townsend, *Boundaries: When to Say Yes How to Say No to Take Control of Your Life* (Grand Rapids, MI: Zondervan, 2017), 199.

CHAPTER 8:

1. Heiner, Dustin, *How to Quit Your Job with Rental Properties: A Step-by-Step Guide to UNLOCKING Passive Income by Investing in Real Estate* (self-pub. 2016), paperback.
2. Matthew 25:23 (*The Living Bible*).
3. Matthew 25:27 (*The Living Bible*).
4. Matthew 25:29 (*The Living Bible*).

CHAPTER 9:

1. Halver, Blair, *5 Hours to Wealth: The Ultimate Shortcut to Lifelong Passive Income and Wealth in Just 5 Hours per Week* (self-pub. 2013), e-book.
2. Matthew 25:23 (*The Living Bible*).
3. Matthew 25:29 (*The Living Bible*).

CHAPTER 10:

1. Luke 16:1 (*The Living Bible*).
2. Luke 16:2 (*The Living Bible*).
3. Luke 16:8 (*The Living Bible*).
4. Luke 16:10 (*The Living Bible*).
5. Luke 16:13–14 (*The Living Bible*).
6. Paschal, Robert, *Subject 2 How to Buy Property with No Credit or Money Down* (Whitchurch-Stouffville, ON: Black Card Books, 2022), 51.

7. Goddard, Neville, *The Power of Awareness* (New York, NY: Noah Press, 2022), 391.

8. Matthew 25:23 (*The Living Bible*).

9. Matthew 25:29 (*The Living Bible*).

CHAPTER 11:

1. Thatcher, Margret, "Thatcher—No One Would Remember the Good Samaritan If He'd Only Had Good Intentions," TransferringData, January 29, 2021, educational video, 0:09 to 0:14 https://www.youtube.com/watch?v=QDF6blmU3co.

2. Luke 10:35 (*The Living Bible*).

3. Shetty, Jay, "On Purpose with Jay Shetty," *Dr. Zach Bush ON: Science Based Approach to Healing Your Gut & How to Prevent Disease with Nutrition* released July 3, 2023, 1hr. 18 min., https://podcasts.apple.com/us/podcast/dr-zach-bush-on-science-based-approach-to-healing-your/id1450994021?i=1000619100808.

4. Cloud, Henry, and John Townsend, *Boundaries: When to Say Yes How to Say No to Take Control of Your Life* (Grand Rapids, MI: Zondervan, 2017), 230.

5. Townsend, John, *Hiding from Love: How to Change the Withdrawal Patterns That Isolate and Imprison You* (Grand Rapids, MI: Zondervan, 1996), 76.

6. Baker, Jim, *How Heaven Invades Your Finances: Book 1: Build the Foundation for Supernatural Finances* (New York, NY: CreateSpace, 2015), 70.

7. Ibid, 78.

8. Heatley, Bill, *The Gift of Work: Spiritual Disciplines for the Workplace* (Carol Stream, IL: NavPress, 2015), 37.

9. Townsend, John, *Hiding from Love: How to Change the Withdrawal Patterns That Isolate and Imprison You* (Grand Rapids, MI: Zondervan, 1996), 63.

10. John 15:1–5 (*The Living Bible*).

11. 1 Timothy 6:10 (*The Living Bible*).

12. Keller, Timothy, Andy Crouch, and Cathie Wood, *Faith Driven Investing: Every Investment Has Impact—What's Yours?* (Carol Stream, IL: Tyndale House, 2022), 37.

13. Ibid, 43.

14. Keller, Timothy, Andy Crouch, and Cathie Wood, *Faith Driven Investing: Every Investment Has Impact—What's Yours?* (Carol Stream, IL: Tyndale House, 2022), 119.

15. Baker, Jim, *How Heaven Invades Your Finances: Book 1: Build the Foundation for Supernatural Finances* (New York, NY: CreateSpace, 2015), 104.

16. Keller, Timothy, Andy Crouch, and Cathie Wood, *Faith Driven Investing: Every Investment Has Impact—What's Yours?* (Carol Stream, IL: Tyndale House, 2022), 29.

17. Baker, Jim, *How Heaven Invades Your Finances: Book 1: Build the Foundation for Supernatural Finances* (New York, NY: CreateSpace, 2015), 43.

18. 2 Corinthians 9:7 (*The Living Bible*).

19. Keller, Timothy, Andy Crouch, and Cathie Wood, *Faith Driven Investing: Every Investment Has Impact—What's Yours?* (Carol Stream, IL: Tyndale House, 2022), 32.

20. Baker, Jim, *How Heaven Invades Your Finances: Book 1: Build the Foundation for Supernatural Finances* (New York, NY: CreateSpace, 2015), 106.

21. Chopra, Deepak, *Seven Spiritual Laws of Success* (Carlsbad, CA: Hay House, 2008), 33.

22. BeBoss, "Kobe Bryant—Get Over Yourself—Motivational Speech," Facebook, February 25, 2020, https://www.facebook.com/bebossfp/videos/3018163934882308/.

CHAPTER 12:

1. Mazzuchin, Peter, *The Spiritual Real Estate Investors Bible: 31 Principles to Ensure Financial and Lifestyle Freedom* (Highland Heights, OH: 10-10-10, 2022), 116.

2. Healey, Bill, *The Gift of Work: Spiritual Disciplines for the Workplace* (Carol Stream, IL: NavPress, 2015), 138.

3. Ibid, 109.

4. Sweet, Leonard, *The Jesus Prescription for a Healthy Life* (Nashville, TN: ADNDP—Abingdon Press, 1996), 194.

5. Heschel, Abraham Joshua, *The Sabbath (FSG Classics)* (New York, NY: Farrar Straus Giroux, 2005), 22.

6. Heatley, Bill, *The Gift of Work: Spiritual Disciplines for the Workplace* (Carol Stream, IL: NavPress, 2015) 37.

7. Sullivan, Dan, and Benjamin Hardy, *Who Not How: The Formula to Achieve Bigger Goals Through Accelerating Teamwork* (Carlsbad, CA: Hay House Business, 2020), 121.

8. Burchard, Brendon, *The Six Habits of Growth*, read by Brendon Burchard (Audible Originals, 2022), audio, 5 hours 4 minutes.

9. Keller, Timothy, Andy Crouch, and Cathie Wood, *Faith Driven Investing: Every Investment Has Impact—What's Yours?* (Carol Stream, IL: Tyndale House, 2022), 38.

CONCLUSION:

1. Keller, Timothy, Andy Crouch, Cathie Wood, *Faith Driven Investing: Every Investment Has Impact—What's Yours?* (Carol Stream, IL: Tyndale House, 2022), 1.

2. LeGrand, Ron, *The Less I Do, the More I Make: Automate or Die, How to Get More Done in Less Time and Take Your Life Back* (Charleston, SC: Advantage Media Group, 2016), 5.

People Over Property

**If you enjoyed my book,
could you do me**

A HUGE FAVOR?

Take a picture of yourself holding my book and tag me on social media using #peopleoverproperty.

I put so much time and effort into writing this book and would absolutely love to see your smiling face holding my book. That would mean the world to me.

Thanks so much!

Ian Lemke